101 Things
You Didn't Know about
SHAKESPEARE

His secret loves!

His artistic feuds!

His biggest flops!

Janet Ware with Al Davis

ADAMS MEDIA
AVON, MASSACHUSETTS

Copyright © 2005, F+W Publications, Inc.
All rights reserved. This book, or parts thereof, may not be reproduced in any form
without permission from the publisher; exceptions are made
for brief excerpts used in published reviews.

Published by Adams Media, an F+W Publications Company
57 Littlefield Street
Avon, MA 02322
www.adamsmedia.com

ISBN: 1-59337-295-7

Printed in Canada.

J I H G F E D C B A

Library of Congress Cataloging-in-Publication Data
Ware, Janet.
101 things you didn't know about Shakespeare / Janet Ware with Al Davis.
        p.   cm.
ISBN 1-59337-295-7
1. Shakespeare, William, 1564-1616. 2. Dramatists, English—Early modern,
1500-1700—Biography. I. Title: One hundred one things you didn't know about
Shakespeare. II. Title: One hundred and one things you didn't know about
Shakespeare. III. Davis, Al. IV. Title.
PR2894.W35 2005
822.3'3—dc22
                                    2005007438

Contains portions of material adapted and abridged from *The Everything® Shakespeare Book*
by Peter Rubie, ©2002, F+W Publications, Inc.

        Interior Illustrations © Nathan Benn/CORBIS

This book is available at quantity discounts for bulk purchases.
For information, please call 1-800-872-5627.

Contents

. . .

To my mom...
            Barbara Ware, who first introduced me to Shakespeare
      by reciting, from memory and without so much as a breath, the
seven ages of man from *As You Like It.*

    Her literary influence led me to a lifelong appreciation of Shake-
speare and the written word.

                                                    Janet Ware

Introduction

"Who's that?" asks Hugh Fennyman about the dashing young man who's just stepped up onstage to oversee the rehearsal for *Romeo and Ethel, the Pirate's Daughter.*

"Nobody," replies Philip Henslowe. "He's the author."

This scene from the 1998 movie *Shakespeare in Love* is make-believe, but the scenario it depicts from 1593 isn't far from the truth. In his own time, William Shakespeare was unknown to the people who watched his plays. Audiences came to see plays and players. They didn't know who wrote the scenes they saw acted out onstage, nor did they particularly care. My, how times have changed.

No dramatic producer who prizes his professional reputation would dare call William Shakespeare a nobody today. His works are required reading in classrooms the world over, and even if you've never seen one of his plays performed, there's a good chance you know at least one of his characters by name and more than a few of his words by heart.

What's happened over the last 400 or so years to take a struggling Elizabethan playwright from relative obscurity in a backstreet London theater to megafame on the world's most celebrated stages? Plenty.

William Shakespeare started out with neither money nor prestige. The son of a glove maker and minor civic official in a small provincial town, he was entitled to attend grammar school for free, but he never went to college. He married at eighteen, possibly at the end of a shotgun, and shortly after fathering three children, he left his family for London— some say because he was running from the law. He took up with theater folk, considered just a cut above vagabonds and beggars in those days. He hardly seemed destined for success. And yet he became a literary icon.

When he landed in London around 1587, Shakespeare was one of dozens of aspiring young playwrights. But there was something special about this one. He had a knack for clever wordplay and a rare talent for turning old tales into marketable new plays. He also had ambition.

Shakespeare seems never to have courted fame during his lifetime, but his friends made sure he would not be forgotten. Two of them published the first collection of his plays seven years after his death.

William Shakespeare had an ear for the language and an eye for a good story that no writer so far has been able to top. Over the years, many have questioned this playwright's authenticity. That a man with minimal education and virtually no social connections could reach the pinnacle of literary success, these skeptics say, just doesn't add up. Several candidates for the title have been suggested and the controversy continues, but to date, the most evidence is still with the man from Stratford.

There's a lot about William Shakespeare we don't know. We can't help but continue to be curious. For more than four centuries, William Shakespeare's story has fueled our dreams and fed our doubts. Who was this man . . . really? Read on—some surprises may lie ahead.

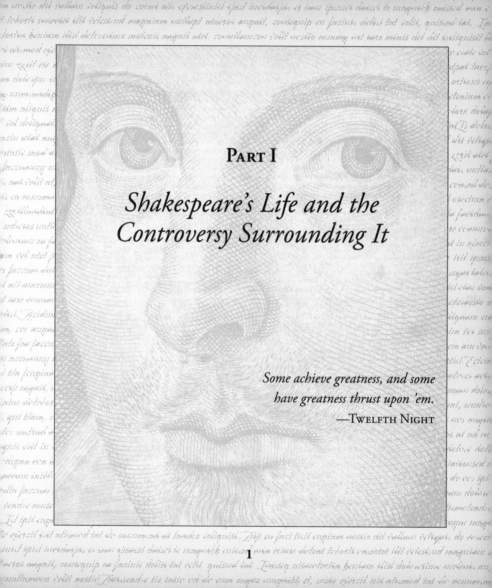

PART I

Shakespeare's Life and the Controversy Surrounding It

Some achieve greatness, and some have greatness thrust upon 'em.
—Twelfth Night

WILL THE REAL WILLIAM SHAKESPEARE PLEASE STAND UP?

FROM OUTWARD APPEARANCES, William Shakespeare did not seem destined for success. He certainly wasn't born to greatness—or even to literacy. His parents couldn't read or write, and he had barely a grammar school education. He rarely spelled his name the same way twice, may have had more than one run-in with the law, and was married quite suddenly in what today we'd call a shotgun wedding.

But what Shakespeare lacked in family background and formal schooling, he made up for in keen observation and natural talent. Not only did he possess an extraordinary understanding of human nature, he had the wherewithal to put it down on paper. Shakespeare's skill with words delighted theater audiences of his day and he died a wealthy man. End of story.

Well, not quite. Long after he was dead and subsequently elevated to icon status, rumors began to circulate. We'll never know for sure which of his plays were well received during his time and which "flopped" (records from those days just aren't sufficient). Ultimately, perhaps Shakespeare's greatest failure lies in the fact that so many people over the years have questioned whether he even wrote the works that have been attributed to him. The man we know as William Shakespeare couldn't have written all those plays, many have argued. He was too uneducated, too unworldly. Or was he? Only the real William Shakespeare knows, but the controversy continues to rage nearly 400 years later.

⌁ I ⌁

From humble beginnings

By all accounts, William Shakespeare's lineage was pretty unremarkable. He certainly did not have the kind of familial connections that would have advanced his career or catapulted him into high society.

His father, John, was not without talent to advance his fortune in the world, however. The son of tenant farmers, John went into trade—as a glove maker and leather dresser. He must have been good at his craft, because he earned enough to purchase two houses on Henley Street in Stratford-upon-Avon for his combination workshop/home, and to attract one of the area's most eligible bachelorettes.

Mary Arden, daughter of an influential Warwickshire family, was "a good catch" in those days. John's marriage to her around 1557 undoubtedly helped boost his social standing. It certainly boosted his property holdings. Mary brought to the marriage a sixty-acre farm, which John would later mortgage when times got tough. She also brought a less-than-desirable religious heritage. The Ardens were ardent Catholics, which could have proved a liability during the very Protestant Elizabeth I's reign. Mary's Catholic roots may have contributed to the unsubstantiated charge by one of Shakespeare's early biographers that "he died a papist." There's no proof, however, that our playwright practiced Catholicism.

It's quite likely that Shakespeare's parents were illiterate. Literacy in Elizabethan times was defined as the ability to read *and* write. John Shakespeare may have gone to school only long enough to learn to read. Mary, on the other hand, would probably not have attended school at all; most girls did not.

Over the course of his lifetime, John Shakespeare enjoyed a fair amount of prominence in Stratford, but he also occasionally ran afoul of the law. In 1552, he was fined for having his own personal dungheap. But while his failure to use the community's "common muckhill" was almost certainly a serious affront to contemporary sanitation efforts, it apparently wasn't a serious blot on his record. He later went on to a political career, serving first as chamberlain, then burgess, alderman, and finally, high bailiff, a position equal in modern times to mayor.

Around 1576, however, John Shakespeare's life began to unravel. No one knows why exactly, but his fortunes, along with his reputation, suddenly started to wane. He fell into heavy debt—perhaps he'd been tending to politics more than business—and began missing council meetings and Sunday church services. In the early 1570s, his application for a coat of arms, which would have confirmed his rank as a gentleman, was denied. Meanwhile, a relative on his wife's side was brought up on charges of Catholic conspiracy and subsequently lost his head.

We don't know what effect this sad turn of family events might have had on young William. The records of his early years are few and far between. What we do know is that, from humble beginnings, John

Shakespeare's oldest son would go on to achieve the kind of fame now reserved for rock stars and sports legends. Oh, and by the way, that coat of arms John Shakespeare was denied? It was awarded to his son William in 1596. Family honor was restored, and then some. Over the past four centuries, the name William Shakespeare has become the very "household word" the author himself alluded to in *Henry V.*

～2～

A star is born

William Shakespeare came into the world in Stratford, England, on . . . well, the exact date is a matter of debate. As with much of what we know about Shakespeare's early life, the facts surrounding his birth are largely a matter of conjecture. Scholars seem to have arrived at a probable date purely by process of elimination.

Surviving baptismal records tell us that a "Gulielmus filius Johannes Shakspere" (translation: William, son of John Shakespeare) was christened on April 26, 1564, in Holy Trinity Church, Stratford-upon-Avon, county of Warwickshire. It was customary in those days to baptize a child three days after birth. The risk of infectious disease and high infant mortality rates made timely christenings a must. Hence

April 23, 1564, became the officially recognized date of Shakespeare's birth.

April 23 may have also been selected for another reason. It coincides with the feast of St. George, which since 1222 has been celebrated as a national festival in Britain. Because St. George was already the patron saint of England, scholars may have simply deemed it fitting to assign the same birth date to the nation's most revered poet and playwright.

William was the third of eight children born to John and Mary Shakespeare and the oldest one to live past infancy. The first, a daughter named Joan, was baptized in 1558. No record of her death or burial seems to have survived, but given that another Shakespeare daughter was christened Joan eleven years later, it's probably safe to assume the first one died quite young. A second daughter, Margaret, was baptized in December 1562 and buried four months later. The third daughter, Anne, born in 1571, died at the age of seven.

William himself was lucky to have made it past childhood. Within three months of his birth, bubonic plague struck Stratford, killing more than 200 residents—approximately one in seven—including four children in a neighboring house on Henley Street. How baby William managed not to succumb to this dreaded disease remains a mystery. Ultimately, only five of John and Mary Shakespeare's eight children would survive into adulthood. In addition to William, there was Gilbert, born in 1566, the second Joan, who arrived in 1569, then Richard in 1574, and Edmund in 1580. Of these, only Joan outlived William.

Interestingly, Shakespeare was buried on his "birthday," April 23, in 1616. This may have been a lucky coincidence, but considering the way Shakespearean scholars have played fast and loose with many details of the author's life over the centuries, you can't help but question the odds. Could William Shakespeare really have been born and buried on the same date fifty-two years apart?

⌐3⌐

It wasn't the genes

Some families just naturally seem to beget greatness. There are political dynasties like the Kennedys and Roosevelts, acting legacies like the Barrymores. And then there are those otherwise run-of-the-mill families who can lay claim to only one progeny we remember. Such were the Shakespeares. Aside from William, no other person bearing that surname has ever chiseled his or her way into the hearts and minds of their own generation, much less later ones.

It's not as if John and Mary Shakespeare didn't try to create a dynasty. They had eight children, and as mentioned in the previous point, William was the oldest to survive. Two of his sisters died before he was born; a third passed away when he was fifteen. His remaining siblings—three brothers and a sister—seem to have made their way into the history books only by virtue of their older brother's fame. Even then, what we know about Gilbert, Joan, Richard, and Edmund Shakespeare is sketchy.

Gilbert, next in line behind William, was reputedly named for Gilbert Bradley, John Shakespeare's friend and fellow glover. Like his older brother, Gilbert apparently struck out for London to seek his fortune. Records from 1597 show he was a haberdasher of St. Bride's (a churchyard in the heart of London). He later returned to Stratford, where he seems to have had a few run-ins with the law. Never married, he died in 1612.

Joan Shakespeare was a bundle of "onlys": the only daughter to survive childhood, the only Shakespeare sibling besides William to marry, and the only one to outlive her famous brother. Her husband was an obscure hatter named William Hart; they married sometime before 1600 (no record of their wedding survives) and had four children. Hart died in April 1616, a week before his dramatist brother-in-law. Joan lived until 1646.

Of William's brother Richard, we know next to nothing, except that he never married and in 1608 was summoned before the Stratford ecclesiastical court. There's no record of the offense. Perhaps, like his father, he stopped going to church. Richard died in 1613.

Edmund, the baby of the family, apparently took after his eldest brother. As soon as he was old enough, he left Stratford for London to become a professional actor. There's no record of the company he joined, whether he acted in any of his brother's plays, or if he displayed any talent. The one thing we do know is he seems to have fathered an illegitimate son who died in August 1607. Edmund himself died four months later at the age of twenty-seven. He too was unmarried.

William Shakespeare married Anne Hathaway in 1582, and they were the parents of two girls and a boy. Son Hamnet died at eleven, but both of the girls eventually married and had children. But the Shakespeare line was not a long-lasting one. By the turn of the eighteenth century, all of William Shakespeare's direct descendants had died. Descendants of his sister Joan and William Hart survive to this day, but none have astounded the literary world.

~4~
School days, school days . . .

A lot of what we know about Shakespeare the man is pure guesswork. In the absence of records, biographers have been forced to invent details. Take the matter of his education. There's no documentary evidence to prove William Shakespeare had one. But then again, there's no evidence to prove he didn't. The simple fact that he was able to construct such intricate sentences and convoluted plots for presentation onstage seems ample proof that he must have had some formal schooling.

Although education was not mandatory in those days, Will Shakespeare's social standing as the son of a public official would have made him eligible for free schooling. He would have first attended a "petty," or junior, school, where he would have honed his skills in reading and writing basic English before progressing, at around the age of seven, to a grammar school.

Although there's no record to support it, Shakespeare would have probably attended Stratford Grammar School, which had an excellent reputation. His teachers would likely have been Oxford trained, and the education he received there would have been first-rate. This early school experience might have also provided later fuel for his imagination. It's thought that the character of Sir Hugh Evans in *The Merry Wives of Windsor* might have been drawn from Shakespeare's old headmaster, Thomas Jenkins.

A grammar school in late sixteenth-century England was exactly what its name implied. Its sole purpose was to teach grammar—Latin grammar. There was no time for frivolous subjects like art, music, or physical education in Elizabethan classrooms. A typical school day for Shakespeare would have begun at 7 A.M. in winter, 6 A.M. in summer, and ended at 5 P.M., and it would have been devoted entirely to reading, writing, reciting, and speaking in Latin, the language still used in those days for most scholarly works. Along the way, Will would have been trained in rhetoric and logic, and he would have read Latin literature and history. No wonder so many classical references show up in his poetry and plays.

Shakespeare might have also learned a little Greek, and he would have had a full complement of orthodox Protestant religious education, too. He would certainly have studied the Bible and possibly the Prayer Book and *Homilies*. Whether he accepted these teachings is debatable, but he surely absorbed some of their wording. There are allusions to more than forty books of the Bible in his works.

Shakespeare was undoubtedly smart enough to enter a university, and his grammar school education would have prepared him to do so. But he never went to college, possibly because he couldn't scrape together enough tuition money. At about the time Shakespeare might have been applying to a university, his family's fortunes took a turn for the worse. William Shakespeare may have had to close his books and go to work.

ᴄ*5*ᴜ

Shotgun groom?

Perhaps because he penned some of the world's most enduring romances, it seems we long to believe that William Shakespeare lived the life of a romantic himself. Why else would there be so much speculation surrounding his marriage?

Here's what we know for sure: William Shakespeare's wedding took place on November 28, 1582, at Stratford-upon-Avon. The bridegroom, a native of Stratford, was eighteen. The bride, Anne Hathaway, hailed from the neighboring village of Shottery. She was twenty-six and pregnant. The baptism of Susanna, daughter to William and Anne Shakespeare, was recorded just six months after the ceremony, on May 26, 1583.

So was this a shotgun wedding? Did young Will Shakespeare get a slightly older woman pregnant and then do the decent thing to preserve her honor? We can't know for sure, but a few details gleaned by various scholars over the years seem to point in that direction. For one thing, the ceremony appears to have been a rather hasty affair. Instead of the usual three readings of the banns, there was only one; a local bishop had to give his approval for this departure from tradition. Then, too, this pregnant couple's wedding plans might have been put on an extra-fast track because the holiday season was quickly approaching and, in those days, weddings weren't performed between December 2 and January 2.

Some insist that this wedding might not have been rushed at all, that a formal betrothal between Will and Anne could have been made the preceding August. In Elizabethan times, a betrothal was considered as binding as the wedding itself and could thus be consummated. Perhaps these two had intended a November wedding all along and slept together in August to seal the deal?

But there's another twist to this tale. One story going around is that on the day before Will's marriage to Anne Hathaway, a marriage license was issued in Stratford for a certain William Shaxpere of Stratford and an Anne Whateley of Temple Grafton. Could Whateley have been a corrupted version of Hathaway? Stranger things have happened; names were frequently misspelled in those times. But if so, why was she listed as being from Temple Grafton when the Anne Hathaway who married William Shakespeare was from Shottery? Could Shakespeare have pledged his love to a girl named Anne Whateley and given his lust to the woman Anne Hathaway? Could he have been planning to elope with Anne Whateley and leave Anne Hathaway in the lurch? Could Anne Hathaway have gotten pregnant on purpose as a way to trick her young lover into marrying her? She was, after all, twenty-six and well past the prime age for marriage in those days, and she didn't bring property to the marriage. Sounds like a soap opera—or better yet, a plot from one of Shakespeare's later plays.

Of course, we'll never know the answers to these questions; they died with Will and Anne. As mentioned in Number 3, the Shakespeares had three children: Susanna, born in May 1583, and twins, Hamnet and Judith, in February 1585. While they may have lived apart for much of their married life, they remained husband and wife for close to thirty-four years. Anne survived William by seven years and, as far as we know, she did not remarry or take a lover.

6

On the lam?

It's widely accepted that, at some point early in his marriage, William Shakespeare left his wife and three young kids in Stratford and headed for London. The actual date of his departure is not known for certain. Neither is the reason. Some say he was running from the law.

About a year into his marriage, Will might have hooked up with the proverbial "wrong crowd" in Stratford. Legend says he and his new-found "friends" tried poaching some deer on the grounds of Charlecote Park, nobleman Sir Thomas Lucy's estate. Will got caught. As if prosecution for his offense wasn't enough to teach this would-be thief a lesson, Shakespeare seems to have compounded the crime by writing a ballad in which he painted the Lucy family in a less-than-favorable light. He supposedly revealed his talent for punsmanship by using words like "Lowse" and "Lowsey" in place of Lucy and . . . well, you can just imagine how a peer of the realm would have received that. Facing prosecution once more, Shakespeare reportedly felt obliged to drop everything and depart Stratford for London, perhaps even in the dead of night, before he could be hauled off to jail.

Sadly, the original ballad about Sir Thomas Lucy—Shakespeare's first stab at poetry, so the story goes—does not survive. But knockoffs continue to proliferate, as do the legends surrounding this incident.

One has Shakespeare killing rabbits; another finds him nailing his ballad to the gates of Charlecote Park in a bold, Martin Luther–like defiance. None of these, including many details of the original incident that sparked the frenzy, can be verified. The earliest accounts of this supposed chapter in Shakespeare's life date from more than 100 years after the events were supposed to have taken place, and they could be based on the character of Shallow in *The Merry Wives of Windsor*, whom some say is based on Sir Thomas. So, like many incidents in Shakespeare's life, there's a chicken-and-egg dilemma here: Did Shakespeare skewer his old enemy in his plays, or did the plays cause later biographers to infer (and invent) stories of his life?

The fact is, Shakespeare could have gone to London for any number of reasons: to escape an unhappy marriage, to pursue a business opportunity, to see the sights. Maybe he arrived in London simply because an acting troupe with which he had allied himself happened to take him there. Whatever his reason for going, we should be glad he stayed. In London, the William Shakespeare we know and love began to take shape.

~7~

The many "careers" of William Shakespeare

Huge gaps exist in the documented story of William Shakespeare. We know that his wife Anne gave birth to twins in 1585; their baptismal certificates are part of the public record. We also know, from a pamphlet written by rival dramatist Robert Greene, that by 1592 Shakespeare was somewhat prominent in London theater circles. About the seven years in between, however, we know absolutely nothing.

What could Shakespeare possibly have been doing between the ages of twenty-one and twenty-eight? Attempts to answer this question over the centuries have given rise to several larger-than-life legends, many of which center on possible careers Shakespeare might have pursued during these so-called lost years.

To support his family, Will Shakespeare may have tried his hand at a trade, possibly glove-making like his father or perhaps butchery. There is conjecture, too, that he might have been apprenticed to a lawyer or physician. Some of the language in his plays seems to suggest he had a better-than-average working knowledge of both professions.

The reign of Elizabeth I was one of exploration, international diplomacy, and conflict between England and other European powers, especially Spain. Perhaps, like many of his contemporaries, William Shakespeare was a soldier or sailor. Firsthand familiarity with other lands could explain why so many of his plays have foreign settings.

The fact that Shakespeare never attended a university but wrote like a man who did has fueled speculation that he might have served as a schoolmaster or private tutor in some country manor. In addition to income, a teaching position would have given him the opportunity to polish his knowledge of rhetoric and to keep his Latin grammar skills current. Proponents of this theory point to a surviving will, attributed to one Alexander Houghton, that mentions a tutor named "William Shakeshafte" who had connections to the theater. Could Shakeshafte be Shakespeare? It's possible; surname misspellings were common in those days.

It's pretty safe to assume that at some point during the seven lost years, William Shakespeare made his way to London and became involved in the theater, possibly around 1587. Precisely why he relocated is uncertain. Perhaps he joined one of the many touring companies of actors that frequently passed through Stratford. It is unlikely that he would have set out for the city and a career in theater without a connection of some kind.

Although popular legend has him first holding horses at the stage door, it is more widely believed that Shakespeare's earliest job in the theater would have been as a stage manager. He allied himself early on with the Earl of Leicester's Men, where he would have met James Burbage, who built the first public playhouse in London, and his actor son, Richard. Perhaps these two recognized Shakespeare's natural feel for language. They might have encouraged him to hone his craft by editing plays and collaborating with other writers. In any event, by 1592, when the documented story of William Shakespeare resumes, he had already acquired quite a reputation around London as an actor and playwright.

∽ 8 ∼

Player before playwright

William Shakespeare did not enter the realm of theater as a playwright. He was an actor first, a fact that may help to explain why, nearly 400 years after his death, his plays are still being performed. They were that good for the actors and (later) actresses. Shakespeare had mastered stagecraft long before he ever set pen to paper.

Growing up in Stratford, Will would have been exposed to acting and plays early on. Traveling troupes of actors regularly made the rounds of the midland villages in those days; as the son of a public official, Shakespeare would likely have attended several performances, and he may have become enamored of the theatrical life. Some scholars believe that Shakespeare got to London in the first place by joining one of these touring companies.

Of course, becoming an actor wouldn't have been difficult in Shakespeare's time. You certainly didn't need any special training or even previous experience. Securing an acting job was often as simple as being in the right place at the right time. If you happened to show up at the theater on the same day the company lost one of its cast members to accident or illness, you just might get a part. Typically, acting lessons took the form of what today would be called "on-the-job training."

That's not to say acting was an easy way to make a living. To keep theater seats filled, acting companies had to provide a never-ending stream of new material. Not only would actors have to play more than one role in a single production, they would also have to carry the lines for half a dozen plays simultaneously in their heads. On any given day, they might be learning one play in the morning and performing another that afternoon.

Shakespeare never became a bona fide star onstage. Although we don't know exactly which parts he played, we can surmise they were small ones. A surviving cast list for *Sejanus*, a play by his friend Ben Jonson, for example, shows William Shakespeare as one of the players.

At some point (we're not exactly sure just when), Shakespeare shifted his interest from onstage to backstage and began writing full-time. Perhaps he one day had had his fill of mediocre scripts, picked up his pen, and started writing. Judging from the popularity his plays enjoyed, Elizabethan audiences were grateful for the change.

Even after he began making a name for himself as a playwright, Shakespeare continued to appear onstage periodically. Scholars believe he may have sometimes taken cameo roles in his own productions. There have been suggestions, for example, that he played the ghost of the dead king in the original production of *Hamlet* and that he may have portrayed the Chorus in his company's rendition of *King Henry V.* Now wouldn't you just love to have been in the audience for one of those performances?

~ *9* ~

Ah, for the life of a writer

The world has long held romantic notions about the everyday life of its great writers. We imagine the classic authors to be lonely, tortured souls. We picture them with quills in hand, toiling by the light of their candles at rickety desks in drafty garrets located on the seedier sides of London, Paris, or St. Petersburg. These creative geniuses, we surmise, would have been driven to write solely for the sake of their art; they'd have given little or no thought to financial remuneration.

Enter William Shakespeare. Some of his contemporaries labeled this man we call a poetic genius a hack. Yes, Shakespeare was driven to write, but not solely for art's sake. He needed to earn a living, and to do so, he had to write plays people liked. A lot of them.

Few playwrights became rich in Shakespeare's day, nor were they held in the highest esteem. Theater was thought to be one of the lesser arts; on any given day, it ranked right alongside public executions and bear baiting as a preferred choice of entertainment for the masses. A dramatist's work had to satisfy two masters: the censors, who could shut down any production they deemed politically or socially offensive, and the audiences, which were always on the lookout for something new. If you wrote for the theater in Elizabethan times, you had to know just how far you could push the envelope—and you had to be prolific. Shakespeare was both.

Although we can't know for certain exactly how he worked on a day-to-day basis, we can make some good guesses. We know that at the height of his career, he wrote an average of two plays per year, which, considering the complexity of his themes and plots, is a pretty good pace. We know, too, that during this same time he earned approximately £200 a year from his writing, quite respectable at that time and significantly better than most of his contemporaries.

Except for a brief foray into poetry, Shakespeare was primarily a dramatist. In writing for the Elizabethan stage, he had to take into account the physical layout of the theater itself, the abilities of the individual actors who would be bringing his words to life, and a demanding and fickle audience. After all, when you're paying the equivalent of a day's wages for your theater ticket, you expect to be entertained . . . or else.

As for that other myth we have about writers—the one that says they have no heads for business—William Shakespeare is again an exception. As you'll learn in Number 10, this was one writer who recognized a good investment when he saw one. He was a stockholder in his acting companies, and throughout his lifetime he amassed enough money to live out his last years quite comfortably on an estate in Stratford.

⌁ 10 ⌁

A head for business

It's a widely held belief that creative types we've come to admire over the years have rarely been good with figures. They have barely been able to support themselves, let alone a family, and any money they made from their art seemed to slip right through their fingers. They spent it on things like paper and ink, tubes of color and canvases, bottles of absinthe. They drank, smoked, and gambled, kept odd hours, and hung around in bad neighborhoods with less-than-respectable company. In public, they were often rowdy and loud. And they could be contentious, so much so that they were frequently embroiled in fistfights and challenged to duels.

If those were the rules of being creative in centuries past, William Shakespeare was surely the exception. In a day when the majority of theater folk spent the bulk of their free time in taverns, Shakespeare was the consummate professional. He had a job—writing—and he seems to have taken it very seriously. This was no man who simply "dabbled" in the arts. With one glance at his creative output between 1587 and 1613, it's easy to see that Shakespeare understood the value of hard work and consistency. On average, he consistently wrote two, sometimes three, plays a year, for a quarter of a century.

In Shakespeare's day, the only way a writer could make money was to be prolific. This was a work-for-hire world, and the going rate was £4 per play. There were no such things as royalties, copyrights, or residuals. Shakespeare would have been paid only once for *Hamlet*, no matter how many times it was performed or by whom. The acting company that purchased his play could stage it over and over without paying the author a single pound more—unless the playwright owned a share of the company, which Shakespeare did. Furthermore, changes could be made to the original script without his permission, and other playwrights could even steal whole parts of his play. Plagiarism was not a crime in Elizabethan England.

However, showing oneself to be at odds with the prevailing political and religious climate was. A writer in those days had to be smart as well as creative. So while Shakespeare wrote about royalty and politics, he was always careful to couch his opinions in mainstream language and themes. Before any play could go into production, it had to pass muster with the royal censors; Shakespeare's work always did.

At the height of his career, William Shakespeare reportedly earned about £200 per year from his writing, a considerably better-than-average living in turn-of-the-seventeenth-century England, where a workingman's family survived on about £5 per year. But writing wasn't the only source of Shakespeare's income. He also earned money, maybe as much as £150 per year, as a shareholder in his acting company. He was apparently relentless about collecting debts owed to him, too. His name shows up on several tax registers and court documents related to financial disputes. Whatever profits he made went into land and buildings, so that he was eventually able to retire to luxurious digs in Stratford as a wealthy man.

⌒ II ⌒

A question of faith

Was William Shakespeare Catholic? That question has been a matter of debate for centuries, ever since an Oxford cleric named Richard Davies penned the words "he died a papist" in some early biographical notes he made about Shakespeare.

From our twenty-first-century perspective, even the slightest concern about a writer's religion seems silly. William Shakespeare was a great writer. So in the big picture, does it really matter whether he was Catholic or Protestant? Maybe not to us, but to Shakespeare's contemporaries a man's religious proclivities would have been a very big deal. People could be killed in those days for practicing the wrong faith.

To understand the significance of religious denominations in Shakespeare's time, you have to start with Henry VIII, who so badly wanted a male heir he engineered his country's separation from the Catholic Church to obtain a divorce from his first wife, Catherine of Aragon. Catherine, it seemed, had proved a disappointment in the marital bed; she had provided him with only one child, a daughter. Henry already had his eye on Anne Boleyn as the next potential mother of a royal heir. Henry got his divorce and, subsequently, more wives and children, including a son by Jane Seymour. His most lasting legacy, however, would turn out to be the establishment of the Protestant Church of England.

When Henry VIII died, things really started to get interesting, religion-wise. His son Edward VI assumed the throne, and the English Reformation continued unabated. But then along came Mary. Catholic like her mother, Catherine of Aragon, Mary immediately tried to reintroduce Catholicism to England. Her methods, which included executing several hundred Protestants on charges of heresy, earned her the nickname "Bloody Mary." Next up was Elizabeth, daughter of Henry VIII and Anne Boleyn. She had kept a low profile during the reigns of her half-siblings Edward and Mary, but once on the throne, she quickly moved to re-establish Protestantism. If you were Catholic and living in England under Elizabeth I, it was wise to keep your mouth shut about your faith, even though Elizabeth was less inclined to make war on Catholics than some of her advisors. At the same time, Rome was urging English Catholics to revolt against the illegitimate government of the queen who had been born outside of sacramental wedlock.

So now back to our original question. Was William Shakespeare Catholic? We know his mother was. His father may have had similar leanings, but in order to be a public official, he would have had to keep his Catholicism under wraps. There are some who believe that the beginning of John Shakespeare's fall from grace as a successful politician and merchant may have begun when word leaked out about his religion. We don't know for sure. As for his eldest son, there is no firm evidence that William was anything other than a member in good standing of the Church of England. Records indicate that he was baptized a Protestant. The fact that his plays were performed before Queen Elizabeth herself indicates that he enjoyed royal favor. An openly Catholic playwright wouldn't have been so lucky.

⁓ 12 ⁓

No spelling champs here

If you're going to try to get away with a lie, it's best to be mindful of the tiniest details. They're the ones that can trip you up.

Take the case of William Shakespeare, whose name showed up on a lot of legal documents, but was rarely spelled the same way twice. This apparent inattention to detail has for years helped fuel the controversy over who really wrote all those plays and whether a man named William Shakespeare even existed at all.

Let's look at the facts. Consistent spelling wasn't any big deal for Elizabethans. They didn't have access to computer spell-checkers, let alone dictionaries. Spelling was done largely by ear. When filling out a legal document in those days, the public official behind the desk at city hall would have simply written down the name he heard a person say, and the end result would have depended on how clearly that person spoke and how well the clerk heard him. In Will's case, what the clerk heard may have sounded something like "shack-spur." It's no wonder, then, that the surname Shakespeare appeared variously as Shakspere on Will's baptismal certificate, Shagspere on his marriage bond, and Shacksepeare in the body of his will.

But what about William Shakespeare's actual signature? There are six surviving examples of that. All are from legal documents, and not one of them is quite the same. We have Willm Shakp, William Shaksper, Wm Shakspe, William Shakspere, Willm Shakspere, and William Shakspeare. Granted, the documents didn't leave much room for complete signatures, which might explain the abbreviated versions. But you'd think a guy could spell his own last name, wouldn't you? Maybe not. Especially if the name he is spelling isn't his name at all. Does this have the makings of a conspiracy to cover up the identity of the real William Shakespeare? Plenty of people have thought so.

On the title pages of his published works, the author's name consistently appears as "Shakespeare." Those who buy into the whole conspiracy theory contend that the various spellings of "shack-spur" belong to a real man from Stratford whereas *Shakespeare* is a pen name for someone else, the bona fide author of all those brilliant plays.

Some doubters have even made a business out of the various name discrepancies. In 1869, George Wise came out with a book about it—*The Autograph of William Shakespeare . . . Together with 4000 Ways of Spelling the Name According to English Orthography.* This unwieldy title includes such spelling variations as Shaxpere, Shagsbere, Shakesspeare, and, of course, the ever-popular Scheackespyrr. Now wouldn't Will's mom have had fun labeling all his camp clothes with that one?

⁓ *13* ⁓
Did Shakespeare write the Bible, too?

Perhaps you've heard the speculation about a secret code to Christ's identity in several paintings by da Vinci? Well, move over, Leonardo. There are some who think William Shakespeare might well have planted a little code of his own in the King James Bible itself.

It's not so far-fetched to think that Shakespeare might have penned some Bible verses. After all, he was at the height of his career around the time King James I commissioned a group of scholars to translate the Holy Scriptures. The resulting King James Version of the Bible, which first made its appearance in 1611 and continues to be used in some pulpits today, reads like a book of poetry. Who better to make a contribution to these lyrical verses than the leading poet of the day?

Those who subscribe to the belief that Shakespeare may have had a hand in the King James Version point to Psalm 46 as proof. The number forty-six is the key to unlocking this mystery. In 1610, the year Shakespeare would have likely been involved in the revision of this project, he turned—surprise, surprise—forty-six.

Now open a copy of the King James Bible to the Psalm in question and count forty-six words from the beginning. What do you see? The word "shake," right? Okay, now flip to the end of Psalm 46 and, discounting the word "Selah," which is actually a Hebrew word used to indicate a musical pause, start counting backward to forty-six again. You should end up on the word "spear." Shake, spear. Get it?

Was this intentional? Did Shakespeare translate this passage and deliberately leave his mark on it? Or did some other translator plant a cryptographic birthday greeting to his favorite playwright? And who in the world made it his mission to discover if the Bible might contain a hidden Shakespeare code in the first place? Obviously someone with way too much time on his hands, that's for sure.

~ *14* ~

Was Shakespeare gay?

The issue of William Shakespeare's sexual orientation pops up enough to earn a spot in the list of frequently asked questions on the official Web site of the Shakespeare Birthplace Trust. No one's really sure about his sexuality.

We know for certain he had a wife and family. We also know he wrote many plays centered on the joys and tribulations of relationships between men and women. That he gave considerable thought to the subject of carnal love is evident in the language of his scripts, which are replete with sexual innuendo and double entendre.

Some of his sonnets—thought by many to be autobiographical—are addressed to a woman, the so-called "dark lady." From the tone of these verses, it seems obvious that she and the poet had an adulterous affair. But it is from his other sonnets, the ones that clearly speak to a young man, that some scholars have gleaned the notions about Shakespeare's homosexual tendencies. There is nothing overtly sexual about his words; there is certainly no suggestion that his love for this "lovely boy" was ever consummated. Still, Shakespeare's very act of addressing his sonnets, among the best declarations of love in the English language, to a member of the same sex has piqued readers' curiosity and set tongues wagging.

If Shakespeare's apparent fascination with cross-dressing is any indication, it seems that he was more likely bisexual than gay. Sexual ambiguity is a running theme throughout his work. Some of his plays' most passionate scenes involve men playing women playing men. And that's enough to instill a case of serious gender confusion in anyone.

～ *15* ～

Rivals for top billing

William Shakespeare wouldn't have been the only playwright of his time struggling to make a name for himself. Elizabethan audiences had a thirst for new productions, and the competition for top spot among those who labored to provide them ran hot and heavy.

If you've seen the movie *Shakespeare in Love*, you already have some idea of the rivalry between Shakespeare and his chief adversary, Christopher Marlowe (see Number 24). By the time Shakespeare arrived on the London theater scene around 1587, Kit Marlowe had already established himself as a playwright to be reckoned with. This brash, Cambridge-educated poet, who moonlighted as a spy for Her Majesty's secret service, is remembered chiefly for three plays: *Tamburlaine the Great*, *The Jew of Malta*, and *Dr. Faustus*. Some lines from these works bear a striking resemblance to lines in a few of Shakespeare's plays, leading some scholars to question whether the two might have collaborated from time to time or just plain plagiarized from one another. There are those who believe that had he not been tragically killed in a barroom brawl just as his career was taking off in 1593, Marlowe might well have risen above the shadow cast by Shakespeare to achieve real greatness as a playwright and poet. Still others think he might actually have been Shakespeare, but that's a whole other story.

Marlowe's roommate, Thomas Kyd, was also a playwright of some note. His 1589 play, *The Spanish Tragedie*, is credited with launching the Elizabethan genre known as "revenge tragedy." Extremely popular in its time, its style (and to some extent its plot) is said to have been the model for Shakespeare's *Hamlet*. Like Shakespeare, Kyd was not university educated; he seemed, however, to have a particular affinity for stagecraft and an instinctive understanding of tragedy. Sadly, his own life took a tragic turn. In 1593, just eighteen days before Marlowe's death, Kyd was arrested for atheism based on documents found in his rooms. In truth, the evidence probably belonged to his roommate, who made no secret of his atheist leanings. In any event, Kyd was hauled off to prison and tortured, after which he claimed the document was Marlowe's. Kyd was eventually released, but is reported to have never quite recovered from the experience. He died at the age of thirty-six.

Ben Jonson, another potential rival, was among Shakespeare's closest friends. Like Shakespeare, Jonson came from humble roots and was an actor before he became a playwright; he performed the leading role in *The Spanish Tragedie*. Jonson's first play of note, *Every Man in His Humor*, was a box-office bomb, but his later comedies *Volpone* (*The Fox*) and *The Alchemist* would help earn him a second-place spot right behind Shakespeare as the most important English dramatist of the Jacobean period. Jonson and Shakespeare remained friends for more than two decades. Legend has it they shared dinner together one night shortly before Shakespeare died; overindulgence in wine that night may have led to Shakespeare's demise.

No overview of the Elizabethan and Jacobean playwriting scene would be complete without mentioning the peculiar case of Beaumont and Fletcher. Francis Beaumont and John Fletcher were collaborators on at least seven plays, and very likely more, written between 1608 and 1613. They shared a house and, according to rumors, a good deal more. Nevertheless, both came from excellent families and thus gave drama some much-needed respectability during James I's reign. After Beaumont's retirement in 1613, Fletcher continued to write on his own and with other playwrights. He even teamed up with Shakespeare on two works: *Henry VIII* and *The Two Noble Kinsmen*.

~ 16 ~

Beware the Greene-eyed monster

By the time William Shakespeare made his way to London around 1587, the Elizabethan theater world must have closely resembled our twenty-first-century Hollywood. Like modern-day movie scriptwriters, dozens of London playwrights struggled to make a living, each one hoping that this play—or the next, or maybe even the one after that—would be the play to launch him on the road to fame and fortune. In this dog-eat-dog environment, a talent like William Shakespeare's would have been sure to ruffle a few feathers. And the least secure of the lot wouldn't have been able to resist lobbing a potshot or two in the direction of the rookie from Stratford. One such rival was Robert Greene.

Clever and extremely bright, Robert Greene belonged to a group of London playwrights known as the University Wits. They had all come to London from provincial towns by way of Cambridge or Oxford; they were young, rebellious, well educated, and determined to take the theater world by storm. Like his slightly unorthodox friends, Greene fancied himself a kind of intellectual man about town. Mostly he was a dilettante, dabbling in this and that while squandering his talent and the little money he managed to earn from it. He seems to have tried his hand at nearly every kind of writing—poetry, prose, pamphlets, plays—and although he was prolific, he was never particularly successful. Dissolute living seemed to be more his specialty.

While Robert Greene frittered away his time and money on loose women and drink, other writers he knew—like Christopher Marlowe, Thomas Nashe, and that newbie, William Shakespeare—appeared to be doing well. That made Robert Greene bitter. After all, he held an M.A. from Cambridge; Shakespeare hadn't even gone to college.

Shortly before his death in 1592, Greene vented his disappointment and fury. In a pamphlet titled *Greene's Groatsworth of Wit: Bought with a Million of Repentance*, he wrote "there is an upstart crow, beautified with our feathers, that with his Tiger's heart wrapt in a player's hide, supposes he is as well able to bombast out a blank verse as the best of you; and being an absolute Johannes Factotum, is in his own conceit the only Shake-scene in a country."

Scholars have long debated precisely whom Robert Greene intended to single out with this diatribe. Some have argued for Marlowe, and others believe he may have been directing his attack at well-known actor Edward Alleyn. The overriding consensus, however, is that William Shakespeare was the butt of this joke; the "tiger's heart" reference recalls a line from *King Henry VI, Part III*, and the reference to a "Johannes Factotum" indicates that Greene was referring to a jack-of-all-trades ("John do-everything"), which would fit the actor/poet/playwright/theater manager that we believe Shakespeare to have been. Since the pamphlet was published after Greene's death, we can never know for sure. Still, the fact that Henry Chettle, the publisher of Greene's manuscript, subsequently published an apology to William Shakespeare seems to leave little doubt about which of his more successful contemporaries the jealous Greene meant to call the "upstart crow."

⌣ *17* ⌣

And all she got was the second-best bed?

The marriage of William and Anne Shakespeare was probably not a happy one. At least it would appear that way from the few facts we know. There was an age difference of eight years between the two of them and Will may have been a reluctant groom. Anne was already pregnant on the day they tied the knot. Thirteen years into the marriage, the Shakespeares lost a child, their only son. And, though as far as we know, these two never formally separated or divorced, they did live apart—he in London, she in Stratford—for the better part of twenty-five years. (On the other side of the argument, though, he did return to Stratford for his retirement when he could easily have stayed in London.)

The icing on this slightly unorthodox wedding cake came, however, at the end of William Shakespeare's life. According to his last will and testament, Will's wife of thirty-three years was to receive his "second-best bed."

Ouch! The author of *Romeo and Juliet*, the most widely quoted romance of all time, couldn't even leave his wife the best bed? Was he just being mean? Or is it possible he didn't need to be specific about other pieces of furniture because she was entitled to them anyway? Since the law in Shakespeare's time specified that surviving wives would automatically receive one-third of their husbands' estates, the first-best bed may have been hers already. Some scholars with romantic streaks have speculated that this was no slap in the face at all, but rather a sentimental gesture on Will's part. The second-best bed, they contend, was the one in which the two of them slept together and conceived their children.

But even if Shakespeare really did mean to slight his wife with this puzzling bequest, she shouldn't have felt singled out for bad behavior. He didn't leave his younger daughter much of anything either. A month before his death in 1616, Shakespeare changed his will to all but exclude his daughter Judith. In this case, however, the exclusion was anything but mean-spirited. A few weeks before, Judith, then thirty-one, had married a man named Thomas Quiney. The marriage might have been staged to cover up an ugly incident between Quiney and another woman, who had allegedly borne his illegitimate child. In an effort to shield Judith from her unscrupulous husband, Shakespeare left the bulk of his estate to his older daughter, Susanna. Interestingly, that estate included his rather sizable home, New House, where Anne lived after her husband's death and where Susanna and her husband, John Hall, probably shared the "first-best bed."

Shakespeare's will, by the way, made no mention of his literary works, for good reason. They weren't his to bequeath. His playscripts belonged to the acting company that commissioned them; he had no say about their eventual disposition.

And while it was tradition in those days for wives to be interred in the same graves as their husbands, Shakespeare seems to have made sure that Anne would be laid to rest separately. The epitaph on his grave, which he reportedly (but far from certainly) wrote himself, reads [*sic*]:

GOOD FRIEND FOR JESUS SAKE FORBEARE,

TO DIGG THE DUST ENCLOASED HEARE:

BLEST BE Y MAN Y SPARES THES STONES,

AND CURST BE HE Y MOVES MY BONES.

~ 18 ~

The end of the line

When William and Anne Shakespeare married in November 1582, they wasted no time starting a family. As a matter of fact, as already established,

Anne Hathaway was already pregnant with Will's child when she stepped up to the altar. On May 26, 1583, just six months after their wedding, daughter Susanna was christened. The couple's twins, Hamnet and Judith, followed eighteen months later, on February 2, 1585.

There's no way of knowing what kind of childhood the Shakespeare children had, except that pretty much all of it was spent in the absence of their father. Within two years of the birth of his twins, William Shakespeare had relocated to London, presumably leaving Anne to raise the children alone.

Although he may have returned to Stratford for regular visits while his children were growing up, we know of only one time when he most certainly would have come home—August 11, 1596, the day Hamnet, his eleven-and-a-half-year-old son, was buried. We don't know the cause of the boy's untimely death; it could have been an illness, an accident, even the bite of a rabid dog. We can only surmise from the tone of many of the works that followed this tragedy how deeply Shakespeare must have grieved for the loss of his only son. Some scholars have suggested there might be some connection between Hamnet and Hamlet. Could Shakespeare have been talking to the ghost of his son in the opening scene of *Hamlet*? Only the author knows for sure.

Shakespeare was just thirty-two when Hamnet died, but at forty, his wife was past her childbearing years; there would be no son to carry on the Shakespeare name. His three younger brothers would never marry, so when Hamnet died, so too did the surname Shakespeare.

William Shakespeare was buried on April 23, 1616. His wife Anne survived him by only seven years; she died on August 1, 1623. Daughter Susanna's husband, John Hall, passed away in 1635; Susanna followed in 1649. Judith's husband, Thomas Quiney, died in 1655 at age sixty-six. Judith, four years his senior, survived to the ripe old age of seventy-seven. She died in 1662.

Judith bore three sons, one of whom (Shakespeare Quiney) died at six months. The other boys, Richard and Thomas, survived only into their early twenties. Neither had married. Susanna's daughter (and William Shakespeare's granddaughter), Elizabeth Hall, outlived two husbands, but she had no children either. When she died in 1670, the direct line of descent to William Shakespeare died with her.

The only other Shakespeare to marry and have children was William's sister Joan. She and her husband, William Hart, a hatter from Stratford, had four children, descendants of whom are living today.

⌐ *19* ⌐

Final curtain call

Around 1611, William Shakespeare began spending less time in London and more at New Place, the swanky home he had purchased in his hometown nearly a decade before. The second largest house in Stratford, it had once belonged to Sir Hugh Clopton, one of the town's most prominent citizens and a former lord mayor of London. Drawings from the period depict New Place as having three stories and five gables. It was warmed by more than ten fireplaces, which meant there were probably many more rooms; fireplaces in those times were taxable and thus would have been kept to a minimum. The extensive grounds included formal gardens, two orchards, a chapel, two barns, and servants' quarters. That Shakespeare could afford to live in such luxury was indicative of the financial success he attained from a lifetime of work. It was also quite a step up from his birthplace, a few blocks away on Henley Street.

Exactly how Shakespeare spent his time in the five years preceding his death is unknown. Some have called this period a retirement, but it was more like a simple disengagement from the busy London theater scene. He was no longer involved with the theater on a day-to-day basis, but he still had contacts there. Until his death in 1616, Shakespeare continued to make occasional trips from Stratford to London to attend to business involving his acting company, which remained his chief income source. After all, there were no such things as pensions or 401(k) plans in those days. And unlike modern-day freelance writers, Will wouldn't have had an IRA either. He needed to keep working.

Shakespeare penned the last of his plays, *The Two Noble Kinsmen*, a collaborative effort with his friend John Fletcher, in 1613. After that, who knows? Maybe he puttered a little in one of his gardens or spent time bouncing granddaughter Elizabeth on his knee. We know he remained active in local real-estate transactions. A surviving 1614 document, concerning a controversy over the enclosure of some common land in which he had a share, bears his name.

On February 10, 1616, he would have probably attended his daughter Judith's wedding to Thomas Quiney, a local vintner, and he may have witnessed the burial of his brother-in-law William Hart on April 17. A week later he would be buried himself.

Shakespeare was just fifty-two when he died. We don't know the state of his health in those last months, but we do know that on March 25, 1616, he summoned his lawyer and made changes to his will. In the text of this document he described himself as being "in perfect health & memorie, god be praysed." This might have been wishful thinking. Perhaps he was already suffering symptoms of an illness that would kill him.

Although there is speculation that Shakespeare returned weakened in early April from a trip to London, the exact cause of his death is unknown. Some say it occurred following a dinner with Ben Jonson and some other theater friends, where he drank a little too much wine. It seems he simply faded away, a rather pedestrian end for a poet and playwright whose work we're still reading centuries later.

Among folks who thrive on conspiracy and intrigue, there has been the suggestion that Shakespeare was murdered. They say his puffy appearance in the bust above his grave, which was supposedly cast from his death mask, is a sure sign of an arsenic overdose. No proof has been found to substantiate that claim.

~20~

Just a regular guy

If you had lived in London in the late 1500s, would you have wanted to hang out with William Shakespeare? He probably would have been pretty good company. The lines from his plays tell us he had a dry wit and a slightly satiric outlook on life. And despite the fact that he'd never been to college, he was well read, politically savvy, and pretty darn smart to boot.

As a writer, he would no doubt have been keenly interested in people. In a crowded room, he might have kept to himself, preferring to observe rather than mingle, although the bawdiness in his scripts suggests that he would have been able to tell a good joke. He was probably a good listener, too. In all likelihood, he'd have been more intent on keeping his eye fixed on mannerisms and his ear tuned for speech patterns he could possibly replicate in his plays than he would have been in monopolizing the conversation.

Although it's hard to tell from the portraits that survive, William Shakespeare might have been considered quite handsome in his day. His most famous likeness—the one that appears on souvenir bags and in the background of this book's cover—is known as the Droeshout Engraving. The face seems somehow a little too somber and stiff for how we imagine a clever man like Shakespeare to be. This portrait may or not be a reasonable facsimile of the real William Shakespeare. The artist, Martin Droeshout, likely never met the man; he was just fifteen when Shakespeare died.

The bust of William Shakespeare that overlooks his grave in Holy Trinity Church at Stratford-upon-Avon isn't much more appealing, although it may be a good deal closer to the real thing. It was supposedly made from Shakespeare's death mask. If so, he'd either put on a few pounds in his declining years or he suffered from dropsy. His facial features are quite puffy.

By far the friendliest portrayal is the Chandos Portrait, otherwise known as "guy with a gold earring." Attributed to the artist John Taylor, it is believed to have been painted from life. Not all elements are original, however. The shirt collar and beard have been retouched, and the earring was added later. This painting came to be known as the Chandos Portrait because, after changing owners several times over the years, it finally ended up in the hands of the Duke of Chandos. Sometime later, it was passed to the Duke of Ellesmere, who in 1856 donated it to London's National Portrait Gallery. It remains in the collections there, but is currently not on display. You can see it by accessing the museum's Web site (*www.npg.org.uk*).

If you think you might have enjoyed getting to know William Shakespeare up close and personal, the Chandos Portrait is most definitely worth a look. Chisel off a few pounds, add a little more hair on top, and you can *almost* see Joseph Fiennes as he appeared in the 1998 movie *Shakespeare in Love*. Well, at least the earring is the same.

⌐ 21 ⌐

Come out, come out wherever you are!

Imagine you're a writer who's had a fair amount of success in life. So what that you didn't go to college and you came from humble stock? You've earned a decent living, your work has been well received, and, hey, words you wrote are on everybody's tongues these days. What more could a writer want?

Now imagine someone accuses you of being a fraud. Or worse yet, claims you never existed at all. He argues that a minimally educated country bumpkin couldn't possibly have written all those plays or invented so many clever turns of phrase. Someone else must have done the writing. You know he's wrong; you know the work is yours. But you can't prove it. Because you died long before the controversy ever began.

Welcome to the world of William Shakespeare. For better than 200 years, the poet and playwright we've come to revere as a literary icon has been the focus of an authorship debate that just won't quit.

No one seems to have questioned Shakespeare's authorship while he was still writing, and by the time they did, he was no longer around to defend himself. Surely, for a hard-working, likeable, financially solvent writer like Will Shakespeare this would have seemed, to quote from *Julius Caesar*, "the most unkindest cut of all." How could people possibly not believe he authored all those plays?

Well, there was that matter of his education for one thing. He never progressed beyond grammar school, which means his formal education would have ended around fourteen. Yet Shakespeare used a lot of big words in his works, many of which were brand-new to Elizabethan audiences. He made numerous references to classical history and literature. And he seemed to know an awful lot about foreign countries and courtly manners. How could a small-town guy with no college degree be so erudite and worldly? How could he know so much? Perhaps because in grammar school, where he would have studied Latin and Greek, Shakespeare also learned the value of scholarly research?

There are those, too, who argue that, while sixteenth- and seventeenth-century records bearing Shakespeare's name still exist around Stratford, not one of them, aside from his gravestone, identifies the man as a writer. And why would they? Shakespeare made his name in London. Would the locals have known—or cared—what he did there?

But if Shakespeare didn't write Shakespeare, who did? Over the years, several names have been proposed. Leading contenders, like Christopher Marlowe, Sir Francis Bacon, and Edward de Vere, the seventeenth Earl of Oxford, seem halfway plausible. Others, like Queen Elizabeth I, are downright absurd. Besides, if Shakespeare the minor actor was simply a front for the real person who penned the greatest plays of all time, surely someone would have spilled the beans before now. Seventeenth-century London wasn't that big . . . or that discreet.

What is it about Shakespeare's success that compels us to doubt his authenticity? Certainly, many people think the Shakespearean body of work is too good to be true, and we know that anything too good to be true usually isn't. So the controversy will continue, despite the consensus of scholars that Shakespeare of Stratford actually did write the plays and poetry that continue to be read and admired.

⁓ 22 ⁓

And in this corner . . .

Questions about whether Shakespeare really wrote Shakespeare began to surface as early as 1785. Most of these were fueled by social snobbery. At this point, many academics believed that a country lad with only a grammar school education could not have written such lyrical poetry and prose.

By the late eighteenth century, Shakespeare had already assumed a larger-than-life reputation, so it was probably with some reluctance that the initial doubters stepped forward to state their case. But no sooner had a few brave souls cracked the door than others leaped up to open it wide. Names we know, such as Mark Twain, Sigmund Freud, Ralph Waldo Emerson, Walt Whitman, Helen Keller, and Orson Welles, all weighed in on the topic of Shakespeare's authorship, and many scurried to line up behind their favorite candidates.

More than fifty names—some plausible and some downright ridiculous—have been suggested over the years as likely authors of Shakespeare's works. The leading serious contenders for this crown remain:

- **Sir Francis Bacon, English philosopher, essayist, and statesman.** His chief booster appears to have been the American Delia Bacon (no relation to Sir Francis, although she may have come to think so later in life). In 1857, she published a book arguing that Bacon was Shakespeare and managed to enlist a host of followers, including noted American author Nathaniel Hawthorne, who later disavowed their connection. While relatively successful in generating backers for the cause, Delia seems to have carried her research a tad too far. After attempting to open Shakespeare's tomb, she was committed to an asylum near Stratford.

- **Christopher "Kit" Marlowe, Elizabethan playwright and Shakespeare's contemporary.** Marlowe's obvious talent for dialogue and stagecraft would have made him the leading choice to be Shakespeare, except for one thing: He died in 1593. William Shakespeare continued to write for another twenty years. The only way Marlowe could have been Shakespeare is if he faked his own death; some believe that's exactly what he did.

- **Edward de Vere, seventeenth Earl of Oxford.** A large cult of backers, who call themselves "Oxfordians," has emerged to support the claim that this sixteenth-century nobleman was the man behind the name William Shakespeare. Born to a life of privilege, he would have had access to books and education, and he might have visited many of the places Shakespeare used as settings for his plays. Like Marlowe, though, Edward de Vere died well before Shakespeare had penned his last play in 1613. Supporters of the earl's authorship insist that he wrote all of the plays we attribute to Shakespeare before he died, making arrangements for their release at a later date.

Today, the authorship controversy continues to rage, and you can't help but wonder why. No one seems to care whether Dante really wrote *The Inferno* or if Homer was a pen name. What is it about William Shakespeare that so tickles our curiosity and skepticism?

~ 23 ~

Face-off between two camps

When it comes to identifying the actual person who wrote such master-pieces as *The Merchant of Venice*, *Twelfth Night*, *Hamlet*, and *Othello*, the so-called experts—folks who have made entire careers out of studying the works of Shakespeare—fall into two broad camps: the Oxfordians and the Stratfordians. In a nutshell, the Stratfordians think Shakespeare wrote Shakespeare; the Oxfordians think it was more likely Edward de Vere, the seventeenth Earl of Oxford (see Number 22). Each side believes it has the conclusive proof.

The Stratfordians stand solidly behind their hometown boy. They brush aside Oxfordian arguments that focus on Shakespeare's humble background and his lack of higher education, responding with claims of their own. They say things like "Ever heard of innate talent or natural ability?" and "Who says someone can't develop an extensive vocabulary on his own or write about Italy even if he's never been there?"

Perhaps the most convincing piece of evidence Stratfordians have to bolster their side is that Edward de Vere died in 1604. Ha, ha . . . so there! The Earl of Oxford couldn't have been Shakespeare because Shakespeare was still writing in 1605 and well beyond. Just try and get around that, you, you . . . Oxfordians!

Get around it they do—well, sort of. The Oxfordians concede the death of their hero in 1604. But guess what? Like the schoolboy who knew he'd be absent when his term paper came due, Edward de Vere worked ahead. According to his proponents, the earl stockpiled a whole bunch of plays—*King Lear*, *Macbeth*, *Antony and Cleopatra*, *Cymbeline*, the list goes on—and arranged to have them produced after he was gone. Now that's foresight. What's more, de Vere made sure that any necessary references to contemporary events would be added in his absence after 1604 so the plays would seem current.

"Oh yeah?" The Stratfordians speak up again. "Shakespeare's later plays are obviously more sophisticated than his early ones. He made great strides as a writer over the years. So how do you explain that? Huh? Huh?"

You can see where this is going . . . and it's not toward a resolution anytime soon. On the one side, the Oxfordians are convinced that the "enemy" actively conspires to suppress evidence it knows would prove the pro-Oxford position. For their part, the Stratfordians largely ignore the the other camp's arguments. Stratfordians contend that, given the lack of attention Oxfordians have paid to basic scholarship so far, their claims that de Vere is Shakespeare simply don't hold water—now or ever.

So who's right and who's wrong? Treatises from both sides continue to be published—and they appear all over the Internet—but neither side has made much headway of late. In fact, it seems that most of these articles and books are more about the other camp than they are about Shakespeare or de Vere.

~ 24 ~

The ghost of Christopher Marlowe

Christopher Marlowe has long been considered Shakespeare's chief rival for the title of pre-eminent Elizabethan playwright. By the time Shakespeare arrived in London, around 1587, Marlowe was already making a name for himself in theater circles. Good-looking and gregarious, he cut quite a dashing figure in the neighborhood taverns, where he hung out with other rising young writers such as Robert Greene, Thomas Nashe, and Thomas Kyd, with whom he also shared lodgings. Marlowe was Cambridge-educated and, like Greene and Nashe, a member of the University Wits. He would have been well acquainted with Shakespeare, too. In fact, scholars have identified similarities in Marlowe and Shakespeare's works, leading some to suspect that one playwright may have been copying from the other.

Later, as the controversy flamed over who really wrote Shakespeare, few gave any thought to Christopher Marlowe. As noted in Number 22, he simply died too soon to be considered seriously. In 1593, at the height of his career, Kit Marlowe was killed in a barroom scuffle. And since many of Shakespeare's most famous masterpieces—*Macbeth*, *Hamlet*, *King Lear*—were written much later, Marlowe couldn't possibly have been Shakespeare. Or could he?

Broadway press agent and would-be historian Calvin Hoffman

always believed he was. Hoffman's book *The Murder of the Man Who Was Shakespeare*, published in the United States in 1955 and now out of print, made the case for Marlowe. According to this author's research, Marlowe didn't die at all in 1593. Rather, he faked his own death and fled England to escape imprisonment and possible execution. It seems that in addition to being a spy for Queen Elizabeth's secret service—a little-known fact about Marlowe that historians have confirmed—he was also an avowed atheist. This would have been a serious charge, possibly punishable by death, in militantly Protestant Elizabethan England.

So if Marlowe didn't die, where did he go? To Italy, of course. There, comfortably ensconced in the cocoon of the Italian Renaissance, Marlowe continued to write plays, then smuggled them back to his patron, Sir Thomas Walsingham in England, who had them recopied in an unidentifiable hand and passed to a front man who—you guessed it—was the actor William Shakespeare.

So strongly did Hoffman believe in his theory that in 1984 he obtained permission to open Sir Thomas Walsingham's tomb in Kent, England. He hoped to unearth a box of scripts that would prove him correct, but all he found were Walsingham's rotted remains. Nevertheless, Hoffman continued to defend his position; he died a few years later still believing he was right. Others have subsequently picked up where Hoffman left off and continue to search for clues. In January 2003, PBS devoted an entire episode of its *Frontline* series to the controversy.

On the pro side, researchers point to Marlowe's university education, his obvious facility with language, and the fact that so many of Shakespeare's later plays are set in Italy, a place about which the exiled Marlowe would have had firsthand knowledge. The anti-Marlowe faction, on the other hand, contends Shakespeare was by far the better writer and he didn't need a college education because he had a natural affinity for words. Marlowe, they say, had absolutely no talent for comedy and he couldn't write memorable lines for women; Shakespeare excelled at both.

And so, nearly 400 years after Shakespeare's death, we're still debating who really wrote all those masterpieces. Was it the country bumpkin from Stratford who had a way with words? Or the university-educated expatriate spy? Stay tuned for further developments.

~ 25 ~
Nobility claims a place

Edward de Vere, the Oxfordian candidate in the ongoing "Who was William Shakespeare, really?" sweepstakes, is even more popular today than Marlowe is. His popularity among anti-Stratfordian elements begs the question: Who was Edward de Vere, besides an earl with a name that sounds more French than English?

As noted in Number 22, he was the seventeenth Earl of Oxford. The son of a nobleman, de Vere was highly intelligent, and he was also a patron of the arts. Edward de Vere entered Cambridge at the age of nine and graduated with a bachelor's degree at just fourteen. Two years later, he earned his master's degree from Oxford University and then went on to London to study law. The heir to a sizable fortune, he seems to have spent a good deal of his time and money on books. Surviving receipts show that he purchased works by Chaucer, Plutarch, Cicero, and Plato. One of his tutors, his uncle Arthur Golding, was a highly respected translator of Ovid. Shakespeare is known to have drawn some of his plots from Ovid.

In addition to reading, the earl apparently dabbled in writing, but like many gentlemen of his day, he would not have wanted his name associated with such a pedestrian pastime. Around 1590, de Vere stopped putting his name on his poems and plays. This withdrawal from open credit has given rise to the theory that, in order to keep his writing in the public eye, he might have enlisted the assistance of a young actor named William Shakespeare to serve as his alter ego.

Among the arguments in favor of the earl as Shakespeare is the contention that many events in his private life paralleled scenes in Shakespeare's plays. He is reputed, for example, to have had a fondness for all things Italian; many of Shakespeare's most popular plays were set in Italy. As a member of the nobility, de Vere would, of course, have had firsthand familiarity with life at court and could easily have incorporated details from that experience into his scripts. There's the matter of his family life as well. The earl's father died when he was just twelve and his mother remarried soon after; he apparently didn't get along very well with his new stepfather. Echoes of *Hamlet*, perhaps?

But there is still the one major sticking point. Edward de Vere died of the plague in 1604; Shakespeare continued writing plays for at least another eight years. Oxfordians explain away this discrepancy, contending the earl may have written plays not performed until after his death, or the plays believed to have been written between 1604 and 1613 were in fact all ready for performance by 1604.

Possibly the main problem with the case for de Vere, though, is the absence of any solid evidence beyond Shakespeare's supposed inadequacy and de Vere's biographical similarities with some Shakespearean characters. Without that evidence, it's going to be difficult to change the minds of the majority.

~26~

A royal pretender to Shakespeare's throne?

Yikes! You'd think a queen would have enough to do without adding scriptwriting to her resume, wouldn't you? Well, not according to one vocal faction of the ongoing authorship debate. It seems a few of the folks out there who are certain Shakespeare didn't really write Shakespeare are pretty sure they know who did. Are you sitting down for this one? It was Queen Elizabeth herself!

That's right. When Elizabeth I asked Will Shakespeare to create a special play featuring Falstaff, her favorite character from *Henry IV, Part I*, she was really talking to herself.

Of course, the people who believe this royal masquerade are convinced they have indisputable evidence to back up their claim. Have you ever looked closely at a portrait of Queen Elizabeth I? She had the same receding hairline as William Shakespeare. In fact, if you were to line up the Droeshout Engraving of Shakespeare with a portrait of Elizabeth painted by George Gower, circa 1588, these theorists argue, you might be surprised to find the features of both are not only perfectly matched, but positioned the identical distances apart. Surely that's no accident.

Supporters of the Elizabeth-is-Shakespeare theory further contend that many details in the plays themselves point to the certainty of a female author. "The great characters in Shakespeare's plays are all women," writes George Elliott Sweet, the author of several articles on the authorship question. "All the men have various failings, and that's exactly what an educated, feminist woman would have put in her plays." Well, there you have it. The only educated feminist in Shakespeare's time would have had to have been the Queen. Ordinary women rarely even learned to read and write, let alone labor at literature. Besides, who else would have been capable of writing so knowledgeably about court life except an authentic insider?

But why would the Queen choose Shakespeare and not some other writer of the day to front for her literary ambitions? Because he had the perfect name, of course. It seems that Queen Elizabeth once spoke about "swaying the scepter" in a speech before Parliament. Shake spear? Swaying the scepter? It has to be the same thing, right?

Of course no self-respecting benevolent monarch would have requested this kind of subterfuge from a subject without providing something in return. Rumor has it that Shakespeare received a regular salary from the Queen as hush money. Then, too, there was that purchase of New Place in 1597. Could a gift from the Queen have provided the down payment? No wonder William Shakespeare left his wife and took off for London. He had an empire to run, and Armadas to defeat!

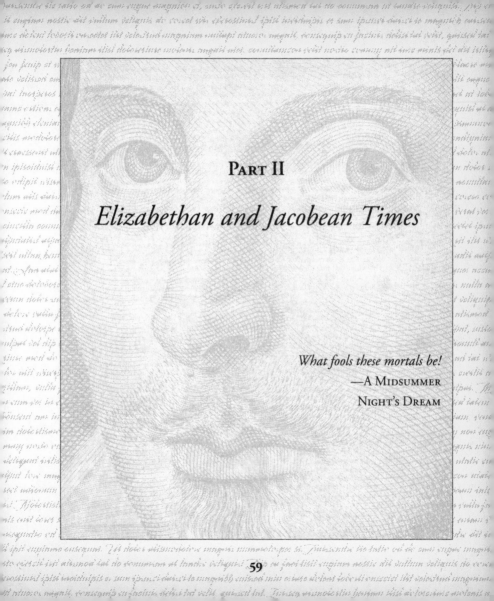

Part II

Elizabethan and Jacobean Times

What fools these mortals be!
—A Midsummer
Night's Dream

Life, Love, and Laughter
in Shakespeare's Day

A writer's work cannot easily be separated from the environment in which it was created. Customs and mores—the limits on what we consider acceptable behavior—change drastically over time. Even our everyday vocabulary may be different from one generation to the next. Idiomatic expressions go in and out of style, definitions change. A word or concept we found offensive when the writer penned it fifty or 100 years ago may now be thought of as downright civilized, and vice versa. If you fully want to appreciate what a writer from another century was trying to say, you can't ignore the events or the environment around which he or she tried to say it.

That's especially true of Shakespeare. Although his work often has been taken out of context, you'll find it easier to read or watch if you know something about the times in which he lived and worked. The strong feelings Elizabethans had about religion, the way they treated minorities—including Jews, blacks, and women—current events, and even healthcare all had an influence on Shakespeare's work. There's the matter of the theater in Shakespeare's day, too. Some knowledge about how plays were written, staged, and watched in those turbulent times can make your twenty-first-century Shakespeare experience much more rewarding.

~ 27 ~

The world from Shakespeare's vantage point

From our perspective in the twenty-first century, the world into which William Shakespeare was born looks slow-paced and primitive. Yet to the people who were already alive in the year 1564, planet Earth may have seemed a frantic and unsettling place. So many things were happening at once. Great changes were afoot in the realms of religion, foreign affairs, and social development.

Why, just twenty years before baby boy Shakespeare made his appearance on the scene, an upstart astronomer from Poland named Copernicus had shocked the Church with his suggestion that Earth was *not* the center of the universe. In Russia, Ivan the Terrible ruled with an iron hand, crushing the nobles, doubling the size of his empire, and giving rise to an elite force of fighting men known as the Cossacks. Further to the east, in China, the Ming dynasty was still in charge as it had been for nearly 300 years and was continuing to make unprecedented strides in cultural development. Great libraries were being established, literature and drama flourished, and impressive art collections were being gathered.

Western Europe, on the other hand, seemed stuck in a rut. Across the channel in France, kings were being assassinated right and left, as a bloody religious war was waged between Catholics and Protestants. It would be another eighty years before the Sun King, Louis XIV, would ascend to the throne and begin shaping France into a bastion of high fashion and decadent pastries. In 1564, Spain was still the major European power to be reckoned with, but she was beginning to show signs of wear and tear. In another fifteen years, Holland would finally stand up to her and declare independence.

Meanwhile, in England, things were looking up. Bloody Mary was no longer on the throne. Her half-sister Elizabeth had taken the reins, and the Protestant Reformation that their father Henry VIII had started was undergoing some rejuvenation. There were signs, too, pointing to England's emergence as a major player in the settlement of some newly acquired lands across the Atlantic. Tongues would soon begin wagging with news about Sir Francis Drake's exploits. By the time Shakespeare turned fifteen, the daring navigator would explore the California coastline as part of his celebrated circumnavigation of the globe. In another nine years, he would help defeat the Spanish Armada, thus securing Queen Elizabeth's favor and his country's place in naval history.

Meanwhile, Sir Walter Raleigh was beginning to make a name for himself as the sponsor of a colony on Roanoke Island, off the coast of what is now North Carolina. It would prove a dismal failure. By 1590, all 117 of the original settlers had mysteriously vanished; to this day, no one knows why. Raleigh himself didn't fare so well either. He fell out of favor after Queen Elizabeth died and was executed for treason in 1618. The colonization of the New World continued unabated, however. The first permanent English colony in North America took root at Jamestown,

Virginia, when Shakespeare was still in his forties, and England was fast becoming a world power.

~ 28 ~

From whence he hailed

William Shakespeare may have spent his most productive years in London, but Stratford-upon-Avon will forever be remembered as his hometown. He was born there in 1564 and educated in the local grammar school. The parish church was the scene of his wedding, and the christenings of his three children. He later bought property in and around Stratford, and when it came time to retire, he settled in the town's second largest house, where he died in 1616. His birthplace on Henley Street is today a national historic site.

If Shakespeare could pay a visit to this town tomorrow, he'd probably recognize the home of his birth, but little else. Modern-day Stratford is very different from the one he knew; in fact, it was already beginning to change in his lifetime. Two fires, a near famine, religious unrest, and the plague all took their toll on sixteenth-century Stratford.

In Shakespeare's time, Stratford was a peaceful little town, famous for its fairs and bustling weekly market. The shops of cobblers, tailors, tinsmiths, butchers, blacksmiths, wheelwrights, and glovemakers (including Shakespeare's own father) lined the narrow, winding streets. On Thursdays, market day, the streets teemed with buyers and sellers. Outside the village, the surrounding farmlands were ideally suited for growing barley, which in turn gave rise to Stratford's chief industry, malting—the roasting and grinding of grain for brewing beer and ale.

Strategically located at a crossroads on the Avon River, Stratford was, in Shakespeare's time, two days away from London by horseback and four days on foot. Although isolated from the big city, the town was not immune to urban problems. On the day of Shakespeare's birth in 1564, Stratford's population numbered around 1,500. Within a few weeks, it had dropped by 15 percent, as whole households succumbed to an outbreak of bubonic plague. A disaster of a different sort struck the town when serious fires broke out in 1594 and 1595. At least 120 houses, one quarter of the existing inventory, burned to the ground. And as if fire and plague weren't enough, famine also tried to rear its ugly head. Heavy rains in three successive years all but wiped out the grain crop; the resulting food shortages led to protests and riots in 1597.

Shakespeare's time was also one of religious upheaval. At one extreme, there were the Catholics, who wanted to continue worshiping in the old ways. At the other end stood the Puritan Reformists, eager to quash the Papist faith—and any similarities included in the English church. The Puritans were bent on exerting their control over every aspect of Elizabethan life, including individual morals.

In between was the Church of England, founded by Elizabeth's father, Henry VIII. Like every other English town, Stratford experienced tension among religious camps, and it appears that Shakespeare's father, a closet Catholic, was caught in the crosshairs. His political and economic fortunes took a nosedive around 1576, and many think his religious beliefs may have been the root cause.

While the residents of Stratford turned their backs on John Shakespeare, they never stopped exalting his oldest son. William Shakespeare long ago replaced malting as Stratford's biggest business. Today, more than 400 years after the playwright himself walked the streets of Stratford, legions of Shakespeare fans flock to his hometown to pay homage.

~ 29 ~
To London, to London . . .

By modern standards, London would not have been a pleasant place to live in Shakespeare's day. It was dirty, disease-ridden, and downright stinky. The streets were narrow, often muddy, and usually littered with the dung of horses and cows. And since there was no sanitation system, chamber pots were routinely emptied every morning into the streets, along with the offal from the city's butcher shops and the garbage left over from ordinary kitchens. Most of it would have been washed directly into the River Thames. Not a pretty sight.

So why would anyone leave a peaceful little market town like Stratford and head to London? For the same reason so many of today's twenty-somethings still flock to New York, Chicago, Atlanta, and LA. William Shakespeare went to London to seek his fortune.

By the time he arrived in 1587 or so, this capital city was the largest in Europe and bursting at its seams. The population that had numbered about 50,000 residents under Henry VIII only forty years before had swelled to just under a quarter of a million. Nearly all of them were crammed into an area known as the "City," which stretched from Fleet Ditch on the west to the Tower of London on the east and was bordered on the north by a semicircular wall and on the south by the River Thames.

The medieval cathedral of St. Paul's dominated the skyline, and London Bridge, with its twenty graceful arches, spanned the Thames. There was no Buckingham Palace in those days, however. The Queen and her court lived out of town, just up the river at Whitehall in Westminster.

When Shakespeare came to London, the south bank of the Thames may have looked like home, with its grassy fields and room for livestock to graze. But the rapidly expanding population would soon lay claim to this land, too, and the result would be Bankside, where the living, if not easy, was definitely a lot more fun. Since all forms of public entertainment were prohibited within the walls of the City, Bankside became home to the wide variety of amusements that Elizabethans seemed to love.

In theaters, taverns, inns, and brothels, well-to-do Londoners mingled with peddlers, prostitutes, cutthroats, and thieves.

Life could be tough for these city folks all right, but crime was the least of their worries. Epidemics of typhoid, smallpox, and bubonic plague ran rampant in London, and the residents had no idea why. The germ theory of illness had yet to be discovered.

Common sense must have told someone that the plague could be spread from one person to another because, during the 1603 epidemic, the London theaters were shut down. This probably saved some lives, but 23 percent of the city's population still succumbed. Fortunately, Shakespeare was not among them. Perhaps he had an incredibly strong constitution; more likely, he just left town. But despite the drawbacks of city life, Shakespeare must have liked London, smells and all. When the all-clear was given, he returned and remained in residence there until around 1613.

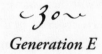

Generation E

The age in which William Shakespeare first flourished takes its name from Elizabeth I, the monarch who ruled England and Ireland during the last half of the sixteenth century. Compared with that of the Elizabeth who currently sits on the throne of England, Elizabeth I's reign of forty-five years was a short one. But this queen, who never married, cast a long shadow over social customs, religious beliefs, parliamentary politics, and even world events.

Elizabeth's ascension to the throne in 1558 must have seemed a breath of fresh air . . . to the Protestants at least. Her half-sister and predecessor Mary Tudor (Mary I) had been an ardent Catholic who tolerated no threats to her faith. In fact, Queen Mary was so determined to re-establish Catholicism in England, she had hundreds of nonbelievers executed, thus earning her place in history, not to mention on many thousands of cocktail menus, as "Bloody Mary."

Although never groomed to become queen (the daughter of Henry VIII and Anne Boleyn, she was in line behind her half-siblings Edward and Mary), Elizabeth seems to have taken to her royal role like a fish to water. She reinstated the Church of England as the official state religion and oversaw the beginnings of her country's rise as a world power.

Judging from her portraits, Elizabeth was quite the snappy dresser. She is most often depicted with her strawberry blonde hair piled high atop her head, sporting heavy ropes of pearls over richly embroidered, voluminous gowns. Elizabeth seems to have enjoyed her power; she waged war as it suited her and encouraged exploration beyond the borders of her empire. But she took time out for fun, too. The well-ordered court calendar of Elizabethan social entertainments included an unceasing array of musical performances, balls, banquets, picnics, and plays, all staged in her honor. If not for the Queen's support, theater in Elizabethan times might have died. Elizabeth enjoyed watching plays, no matter how bawdy, and she regularly stood up against the Puritans and others, who, if given their druthers, would have closed the theaters down.

Shakespeare doesn't seem to have had a particularly close relationship with the Queen. It's not like they were on a first-name basis or anything. Nor does she figure prominently in his work. He refers only once to her directly—in the line "a fair vestal throned by the west" from *A Midsummer Night's Dream*. The indirect reference referring to her baptism at the end of *Henry VIII* may well have been written by his collaborator, John Fletcher, and, in any case, Elizabeth was long dead when this play was probably written. Shakespeare's acting company does, however, seem to have been a particular favorite in royal circles during Elizabeth's reign; it was selected to perform at court more than any other. Legend has it that Elizabeth so enjoyed the character of Falstaff in *Henry IV, Part I*, that she asked Shakespeare to write a play in which the portly and slightly depraved aristocrat falls in love. He apparently obliged with *The Merry Wives of Windsor*.

Shakespeare seems to have viewed his affiliation with Elizabeth as little more than that of employer and employee. When she died in 1603, most poets lamented her passing in flowery elegies. Shakespeare remained oddly silent.

~31~

A day in the life of an Elizabethan

We grouse and complain when the car conks out or the microwave quits. Just imagine what everyday life without modern conveniences would have been like for William Shakespeare.

At least he was a guy, and the son of a property owner, which means he automatically had some educational opportunities and a modicum of independence. He could choose his own spouse and, once married, he wouldn't have been the one saddled with the cooking, cleaning, and kids. If he got tired of small-town living, he could pick up and move to a city, with or without a job. He'd have had some free time, too, for reading and writing or just hanging out in the neighborhood tavern with the guys. Still, his day-to-day existence would have been no bed of roses.

For starters, there would have been no morning cup of coffee, and no designer bottles of water. Beer, wine, and cider, maybe a little fruit juice, would have been his beverages of choice; water, which came from local rivers and streams, was too polluted to drink. Breakfast might have consisted of frumenty (wheat porridge) or flummery (boiled oatmeal) with cream. If he had the money, his breakfast toast would have been white; whole-grain and brown breads were considered second class. Elizabethan kitchens had no stoves or refrigerators, of course; some houses didn't have kitchens at all. Cooking was done over the open hearth, and perishables like meat either were prepared immediately after the animal was slaughtered or were smoked, salted, pickled, or dried for safekeeping.

Like most Elizabethans, Shakespeare would have been a great meat eater. For lunch and dinner, he might have had chicken, pigeon, partridge, or lark, possibly even mutton, venison, veal, or hare, unless it was a meatless day like Wednesday or Saturday. Then he'd have eaten fish or cheese. Meats were prepared in the least time-consuming way; they were boiled. Roasting, which required someone to regularly turn the meat on a spit, took too long. Shakespeare's vegetable choices would have been carrots, cabbage, turnips, and peas, all boiled of course. There were no potatoes or rice; they were too expensive. Dessert might have been a pudding made from milk or stewed peaches, pears, apples, or cherries. Orchard fruits were never eaten raw; raw was considered unhealthy.

Although we don't know much about where Shakespeare stayed in London, we can guess his living quarters would have been dark and sparsely furnished. Lighting would have come from beeswax candles, or tallow, which was cheaper but messy. A fireplace would have provided the only heat. Tables were made from heavy oak and chairs were an oddity; most people sat on stools or benches with no backs. Carpets and upholstery were practically unheard of among the upper class.

While staunch Protestants may have considered cleanliness next to godliness, there were no sinks, showers, or toilets in Elizabethan homes to help them achieve it. Filling a tub with hot water took a lot of time, so Shakespeare probably wouldn't have bathed his entire body very often. He would, however, have trimmed his beard and washed his hands, wrists, face, feet, and hair regularly with perfumed soap. Since he didn't have a toothbrush—they hadn't been invented yet—he'd have cleaned his teeth by rinsing them first in a mixture of vinegar and water, then rubbing them dry with a linen cloth. Although water closets were invented before 1600, they were not in general use, so it's unlikely that Shakespeare would have had one in his youth. When he had to urinate, he'd have used a chamber pot or possibly just aimed for the hearth. And when it came time for bed, he might have nestled down on a mattress stuffed with feathers, but as a playwright, struggling to make ends meet, he'd more likely have slept on straw or wheat chaff.

Worst of all, for those of us addicted to our computers, is the thought that William Shakespeare would have had to do all that writing by hand . . . and with a quill pen no less. A malfunctioning microwave suddenly doesn't seem so bad now, does it?

⁓ 32 ⁓
Grounded in God

Religion was serious business in Shakespeare's time, which may help to explain why he stayed away from the topic in his plays. Still, as a loyal subject of Queen Elizabeth I, William Shakespeare couldn't have avoided at least thinking about religion from time to time.

Elizabethan England had only one officially recognized religion—Christianity. But while the preferred faith may have been undisputed, how a person chose to practice it was not. At the time of Shakespeare's birth in 1564, England was in the midst of a Protestant Reformation that had begun some thirty years before. As discussed in Number 11, prior to the reign of Henry VIII, England had been a staunchly Catholic country. But then the king decided to break with accepted church doctrine concerning marriage and divorce, and the seeds of a whole new set of convictions were sown. Under Henry's successor and son, King Edward VI, Protestantism was openly practiced in England for the first time. Within six years of his ascension, Edward died of tuberculosis, well before the new faith could take firm hold. His half-sister Mary ascended to the throne in 1553, determined to make England a Catholic country again, even if it meant killing hundreds of her subjects to do so. Fortunately—for the sake of the nation's Protestants at least—she lasted only five years on the throne. Under Elizabeth I, the Protestant faith would finally take root and eventually emerge as the Church of England.

Elizabeth approached the re-establishment of Protestantism with a velvet hand, but the idea did not appeal to everyone. Many of those who had grown up practicing Catholicism were not exactly keen on converting. But unlike her half-sister Mary I, Elizabeth didn't force anyone to switch faiths. As long as they worshiped in their own way quietly, she left them alone. But step up to the podium to declare your preference for the Pope loudly and there would be repercussions. Particularly vocal Catholics were regularly fined and sometimes even persecuted, especially during times of political unrest, when their Papist loyalties might be seen as a threat to national security.

At the other extreme was an emerging group of opinionated, militantly Protestant believers called Puritans. Their mission was to promote moral purity and to rid the Church of England of any trappings or rituals that even remotely smacked of Catholicism. Puritan clout continued to grow during the reigns of James I and Charles I. By 1642, the Puritans would help to topple the monarchy briefly and to launch the political career of Oliver Cromwell. The influence of these dissenters was long-lasting, but after 1660 the Church of England would once more assume its place as the country's reigning religious authority.

In Elizabethan times, the subject of religion often split families in two, with Catholics on one side and Protestants on the other. Shakespeare's mother was an ardent Catholic and his father is believed to have had Papist leanings as well (discussed in Part I), which may explain the sudden decline of his prosperous business and political careers. Perhaps he could no longer keep his mouth shut about his faith. If William Shakespeare preferred Catholicism, however, he wisely kept it to himself. A favorite playwright of two Protestant monarchs, he was baptized, married, and buried in the Anglican Church.

~33~
Way beyond readin', writin', and 'rithmetic

For better than two centuries, doubters have argued that the man from Stratford whom we know as William Shakespeare couldn't be the author of the thirty-nine plays we attribute to him. He simply didn't have the education to think so clearly or write so well. It is only when you look closely at what schools were like in Elizabethan England that you begin to appreciate just how flimsy this argument may be.

Think your high school diploma could stand up to one earned in Elizabethan times? Think again. In addition to the required courses you had to take in order to complete high school, you were given the luxury of choosing some electives. Students in Shakespeare's day weren't so lucky. Their curriculum, standardized by King Edward VI to ensure that educated, responsible citizens would be able to carry out the ideals of the Protestant Reformation, didn't allow for individual variations.

Educational excellence in Elizabethan England rested largely on the grammar school, so named because its sole purpose was to teach grammar—Latin grammar. In those days, Latin was not the dead language we think of it as today. It was Europe's universal language, spoken widely among the educated classes and used in law, medicine, commerce, and religion. A thorough knowledge of Latin would have been required not only to conduct business across international borders, but also to practice the Catholic or Protestant faith properly.

Formal education wasn't mandatory when Shakespeare was eligible to enter grammar school at age seven, but as the son of a public official, he would have been entitled to free schooling. On the day he began grammar school, he would have had at least seven years of difficult study ahead of him. There would be no gym classes, art and music lessons, extracurricular activities, or summer vacations. Students reported to school by 7 A.M. (6 A.M. in summer) Monday through Saturday and were dismissed at 5 or 6 P.M. There might be a break in the middle of the day for dinner, but no planned recreational activities would have been part of the routine. And while the school building would have been closed on Sundays, students still weren't free to play. Instead, they would have attended mandatory day-long church services. Their schoolmaster would have been in attendance to make sure they did.

Like the other schoolboys of his day, Shakespeare would have been required to memorize the contents of W. Lily's *Short Introduction to Grammar* in order to be able to read, write, speak, and recite in Latin. As his knowledge of grammar and fluency in the language increased, he would have learned to apply the principles of logic and rhetoric as he tackled works of Plato, Aristotle, Cicero, Seneca, Livy, Plutarch, and Ovid. And he would have been expected to recognize and imitate various great writers. Oh, and by the way, Shakespeare probably would also have learned a smattering of Greek.

Typically, Elizabethan boys completed grammar school by fourteen or fifteen. If they had both money and brains, they would go on to further study at either Cambridge or Oxford University. Shakespeare apparently went to work instead. There is no record that he ever attended a university.

Still, given the grounding that Shakespeare likely received in classical history and literature during his grammar school days, it should come as no surprise that he later showed such affinity for complicated sentences, convoluted plots, and the clever turn of phrase. He didn't need a college degree to show the world he could write.

~34~
It's not what you know

England, even to this day, is a class-conscious society. Unlike the American ideal, which is based on equal opportunity for everyone, England at the time of Shakespeare was focused more on family background than on acquired knowledge or natural talent to determine social standing. As the son of a tradesman, Shakespeare would have been well acquainted early on with his limited opportunities for advancement.

The social hierarchy Shakespeare would have known had its origins in the old feudal system first imposed by William the Conqueror. Beginning in 1066, property in England was doled out to lords and barons who administered the land but delegated farming to the peasants. Lords were responsible for feeding, housing, and protecting the people who served them. In return, their peasants had to be hardworking, obedient, and loyal; there was no such thing as moving from one estate to another in search of a better position. If you were unlucky enough to be born a peasant, you were pretty much stuck in the same place, working for the same lord, for the length of your life.

When the feudal system began to break down, toward the end of the Middle Ages, some attempts were made to dismantle this rigid class structure. During Elizabeth's reign, social position briefly took a backseat to national pride with the defeat of the Spanish Armada. England's economy, however, was still based on agriculture, and when a series of poor harvests in the 1580s and 1590s sparked famines, civil unrest ensued and martial law was imposed for a time. Meanwhile, in an effort to recoup their investments, many wealthy landowners converted their arable land into pastures and, since raising sheep required fewer hands than growing crops, many farm workers lost their jobs, thus triggering a widespread migration to towns, especially London. Perceived as a threat to the prevailing social order, the poor were labeled criminals and subjected to harsh punishments.

The picture was not entirely bleak, however. England's rising prominence on the high seas sparked economic opportunity in the form of such new industries as cloth manufacturing and mining. Soon, instead of two classes, England had three: the nobles and gentlemen; the merchants and yeomen (landowners who farmed their own property); and, at the bottom of the social ladder, apprentices, artisans, servants, and laborers. Shakespeare would have fallen somewhere in the middle.

As a prominent playwright of his day, Shakespeare would have encountered the nobility, including Queen Elizabeth and King James. But he would never have been accepted as an equal. His roots were in the merchant class, and although he would accumulate property and a fair amount of wealth during his lifetime, William Shakespeare would forever remain hopelessly middle-class.

~ *35* ~

Clothes made the man . . . and the woman

If you've ever seen a portrait of Queen Elizabeth I, you have some idea of how fussy the fashions had become by the late sixteenth century. Granted, the Queen would have probably dressed a cut above her subjects; still, even artisans and actors weren't shy about showing a little color and style. And while you might not know your farthingales from your jerkins, you can bet your breeches the Elizabethans did. Fashions were important in Shakespeare's time, especially among men, whose everyday attire outshone that of the women in both color and fabric.

In London, aristocratic men showed off their latest fashion finds by prancing up and down the center aisle of St. Paul's Cathedral every morning between the hours of 10 A.M. and noon; tailors, hoping to secure commissions, would come to take notes. A typical outfit for a well-to-do Elizabethan man would consist of breeches, tight-fitting trousers that reached to just below the knees so that the hose would be visible, along with a series of layers on top. A loose-fitting linen or silk shirt would be worn next to the skin, covered by a close-fitting doublet (another shirt), which would be covered by a jerkin (sleeveless vest). Sleeves were separate garments that attached to the doublet and usually had slits to reveal the layer beneath. A man could dress up or dress down by changing his sleeves. The doublet, made from brocade, velvet, satin, or taffeta, would have likely been a wealthy man's most expensive piece of clothing; doublets were sometimes even mentioned in wills. Accessories for the dapper man would have included a stiff circular collar known as a ruff; a girdle (belt) made from gold, silver, or some expensive fabric; a velvet hat; and either boots or flat-heeled shoes. Underwear, called drawers, was optional. However, most men would wear a codpiece, a fabric pouch that covered the penis outside their breeches. It was usually padded, richly decorated, and sometimes used as a pocket.

Women's clothing was just as complicated, although not as colorful as men's. An ankle-length shift or smock called a chemise was worn closest to the skin. On top of that went a bodice (similar to a man's doublet, but usually low-cut), then a stomacher (a triangular piece stiffened with bone or wood that attached to the bodice front), and finally a floor-length gown, worn open in front to reveal the bodice below. Women's sleeves were also separate, attached to the bodice by ribbons or hooks.

Accessories may have included a ruff, a tippit (short shoulder cape), gloves, undershoes (pumps or slippers), and high-heeled overshoes, to keep a lady's dainty undershoes and skirts out of the mud. Women would have also worn a corset, a bum-barrel (a padded roll tied around the waist under the skirt to hold it out), and a farthingale, a contraption of hoops made from wood, wire, or whalebone worn under the skirt.

With all these layers, it's a wonder anyone could move around at all. The heavily starched, multilayered ruff worn around men and women's necks could sometimes be as wide as nine inches across. At one point, the competition to sport the largest ruff became so fierce that the Queen herself finally had to step in. In 1580, she decreed that anyone attempting to enter London wearing a "monstrous ruff" would be subject to arrest.

~36~
"Humor" *wasn't a synonym for wit*

The people of Shakespeare's time had peculiar notions about the human body. They believed that four bodily fluids—blood, phlegm, black bile (melancholy), and yellow bile (choler)—determined how a person looked, acted, and felt. To ensure perfect health and peace of mind, these four fluids, called *humors*, needed to be present in proper proportion within the body. Of course, since almost no one enjoyed perfect health or contentment in those days, it can only be assumed they must have been experiencing an imbalance of humors somewhere deep inside. Those with persistent ill-health conditions or quirky personality traits were thought to have a predominance of one humor over the other three.

To understand this theory, put yourself in an Elizabethan's shoes and consider an overweight, pale-skinned man who's a little sluggish, maybe even downright dull witted. It's not his fault. He simply has too much phlegm. And that lean, swarthy man over there in the corner who's morose and introspective? He's obviously suffering from an overabundance of black bile. Then there's your neighbor's wife. She's a lusty woman with a cheerful disposition all right, but a touch too impractical. What makes her that way? Too much blood in her system, no doubt. Still, you prefer her to that shrew down the street, the skinny one with the sallow complexion, quick temper, and leap-before-she-looks lifestyle. She's got a real problem—an overdose of yellow bile for sure.

Of course, just because a person was born with the predominance of one humor over another didn't mean he was destined to stay that way. Elizabethans believed the position of the planets and stars could affect a person's humors. So could the time of day, day of the week, season of the year, social position, country of origin, and even what the person had for breakfast or dinner. As a product of his environment, Shakespeare probably would have believed in the theory of humors; he may have even developed character traits based on combinations of the four. And it's pretty safe to assume that when the playwright has Hamlet speaking about a "humorous man," the Danish prince isn't referring to a comedian.

This theory of humors sounds outmoded to us now . . . until you really stop to think about it. Explaining human behavior via bodily fluids is no more outlandish than our twenty-first-century stabs at predicting the future using zodiac signs, palm prints, and tarot cards.

A scourge on your house . . . and then some

In our age of antibiotics and antiseptics, it's hard to imagine how devastating the plague would have been for Elizabethan and Jacobean England. Today, we have drugs to treat it—and we know how to prevent it in the first place. In Shakespeare's day, there was no cure; they didn't even know what caused it. If you or a member of your immediate household contracted this disease in the late 1500s, you were as good as dead.

The worst outbreak of the so-called Black Death originated in China around 1333, then spread across Asia and Europe by way of trade routes. Rats were the original hosts, and when they died, their infected fleas spread the disease to humans. Between 1348 and 1350, approximately one-third of the European population succumbed. By the time this particular outbreak officially ended in 1400, an estimated one-half of Europe's residents had died from the disease. Written accounts from the period suggest the outbreak was primarily of the bubonic variety, characterized by a high fever and painful swellings (buboes) under the arm or in the neck and groin.

Although Europe was never again to experience a pandemic of this magnitude, the plague continued to rear its ugly head from time to time well into the eighteenth century. The combination of overcrowded conditions and poor sanitation provided an ideal breeding ground for the plague. Of course, it would take several centuries for people to make the connection between the disease and their filthy living conditions. In the meantime, they looked upon these periodic outbreaks as signs of God's judgment on the pervasive wickedness of their world.

Plague took its toll on London three times during Shakespeare's life—within weeks of his birth in 1564, then in 1592–1593, and again in 1603. The combined death toll from these three outbreaks, plus a fourth one in 1623, reached 100,000. Fatalities occurred at such a rapid pace that carts were loaded down with corpses, their drivers ringing bells and shouting "bring out your dead." Night after night, the latest victims were collected for burial in common graves.

Public gatherings, including theater performances, were among the victims, too. At the first signs of disease, theaters would be shut down, but whether to prevent the spread of plague by casual contact or simply as a way to impose moral order in a world gone awry remains unclear. Elizabethans may not have yet pinpointed the contagion factor, but many would have recognized the moral depravity of playacting. This single-minded attempt to control the theater didn't seem to have any lasting effect, however. As soon as the danger subsided, the playhouses would be open and thriving once again.

Bleeding was the primary treatment for most debilitating conditions in those days, and the plague was no exception. Rosemary was thought to have some therapeutic effects as well; consequently, it was not unusual to see people with sprigs of the herb sticking out of their ears and noses as protection against catching the disease.

At the height of an outbreak, it would have been easy to trace the path of this disease along London's narrow, winding streets. The windows of households visited by the plague would have been boarded up and branded with large red crosses. No matter that some occupants of the house might yet be healthy. They'd have been locked inside and sealed off anyway, probably never to emerge alive. Cooped up in tight quarters with plague germs and corpses, they didn't stand much of a chance.

~38~

Girls didn't have it so great

Lucky for Shakespeare he wasn't born a girl. Not only would he have been ineligible to attend grammar school; he might not have even learned to read or write. Never mind that a female monarch sat on the British throne. In Elizabethan England, women were second-class citizens; girls hardly counted at all.

Suppose that the Shakespeare born with a gift for getting memorable words down on paper had been Joan instead of her older brother William. Even if she'd been privately tutored and taught to read, she wouldn't have come across many opportunities to use her brains, and she certainly would not have been encouraged to pursue a career. Oh sure, she could have run away from home and headed to London like her brother, but when she got there, she'd have been lucky to secure a position as a scullery maid. If she didn't hook up with a well-to-do family, she'd have had to make her living as a prostitute. She surely couldn't have joined an acting company as did young William. Only men could appear on the stage in those days, and boys whose voices had not yet changed played female roles.

The life of a woman in Elizabethan England was largely predestined by her sex and class. From an early age, girls began on-the-job training in preparation for becoming wives and mothers. They learned "womanly" skills—cooking, cleaning, spinning, milking, childcare—mostly by watching their mothers, helping out with household chores, and caring for younger brothers and sisters. Because marriages were often more about economics than romance, adolescent girls had little or no say in the selection of their prospective mates. Marrying the love of your life was practically unheard of. By the time she turned thirteen, an Elizabethan daughter would likely have been betrothed to a man who could further her father's social, political, or financial ambitions. And that man might have been three times her age, or older.

Once married, usually during her mid-teens, but sometimes as late as twenty-five (Anne Hathaway, remember, was twenty-six), a young woman became the legal property of her husband. If she dared to disagree with or disobey him, she was subject to beating. There were no shelters where a wife could escape her abusive spouse. When violence threatened, a smart woman stayed out of sight and kept her mouth shut. If she'd complained to the authorities, she'd have been punished.

An ordinary Elizabethan woman had no time for recreational pursuits or gossipy lunches with the girls. Her day, which began before sunrise, would have been entirely taken up with mundane tasks of survival: tending the fire, baking the bread, sweeping the floors, milking the cows, emptying the chamber pots. She was expected to bear several children, because so many died in infancy from diseases. She would have had the primary responsibility for rearing them, too. Her day would be a long one, with not a minute to spare, especially for herself. Even if she had learned to read and write, a lot of good it would do her now. She wasn't entitled to an opinion, and her only source of reading material would have been the Bible.

And when she died, likely before the age of fifty, an Elizabethan woman might easily have faded into oblivion. Any letters or diaries she left behind would probably have been discarded. What a woman had to say—even if her surname was Shakespeare—wouldn't have been considered important enough to save.

~ *39* ~
It wasn't easy being different

England wasn't exactly what you'd call a melting pot in Shakespeare's day. In an age when long-distance travel was both difficult and costly, only the wealthy ventured beyond the borders of their home countries for fun. Those few immigrants who made their way to London looking for a better life stood out like the proverbial sore thumbs. Their clothing and customs made them different, and in Elizabethan times, different was something you did not want to be. Jews in particular faced a difficult time.

Under Elizabeth I, England had once again become a Protestant land. If you were a Catholic, you would have been permitted to practice your religion quietly. But if you were a Jew, you would have lived a life of religious subterfuge, observing the rites of your true faith behind locked doors on Friday night and openly attending services at your neighborhood Church of England on Sunday morning.

By the time Elizabeth came to the throne, prejudice against Jews already had a long history in England. During the Middle Ages, Jews were not allowed to own land or practice many trades. By default, they became moneylenders, a career path that could make them wealthy while at the same time earn them the enmity of Christians who came to resent their Jewish neighbors' affluence and peculiar customs. In 1290, King Edward IV officially banished all Jews from the land, a decree that remained in effect for nearly 400 years. To be a practicing Jew in England between 1290 and 1650 was to be a lawbreaker. Those who managed to escape deportation knew they could be kicked out at any time, so they kept a low profile.

Even after Jews were allowed to return to England, around 1650, they weren't exactly welcomed with open arms. Anti-Semitism was deeply ingrained in the British psyche. Church teachings at the time held Jews responsible for the death of Christ, and they were often portrayed in literature and drama as shifty-eyed, hook-nosed, bloodthirsty villains. Shakespeare's Shylock appears to be slightly off the mark in this regard when he delivers some of the most memorable lines ever written on the subject of humanity in *The Merchant of Venice*.

The Jews in Elizabethan London were pretty much left to themselves. As long as they toed the line and pretended to be Christians, they were allowed to eke out relatively comfortable lives as doctors, merchants, and moneylenders. There were no pogroms in England in those days, but there was the unfortunate incident of Dr. Rodrigo Lopez. Queen Elizabeth's trusted physician for many years, Dr. Lopez, a Portuguese immigrant and converted Jew, was accused of plotting to poison her and was executed for treason in 1593. Queen Elizabeth didn't think he was guilty, but she allowed the anti-Semitic climate of the day to prevail nonetheless.

Blacks fared only slightly better in Elizabethan times. To be labeled black in those days did not necessarily mean a person hailed from sub-Saharan Africa. Any dark-skinned person, including those of Middle Eastern descent, commonly called Moors at that time, would have also been considered black.

Due to England's rising pre-eminence as a seafaring power, blacks from Africa and dark-skinned Arabs would have been seen on the streets of Elizabethan London, prompting plenty of stares and whispers as they passed. After all, in an era when upper-class women went to extraordinary measures to keep the sun from even tingeing their pale white skin with color, a black face would have been cause for curiosity.

A few blacks were actually given places in London society, but only as "exotic" servants for the wealthy. Which is all the more reason why Shakespeare's decision to make a man of color the protagonist in his great tragedy *Othello* should be looked upon as revolutionary stuff indeed—as would his villain's manipulative use of racism.

~ 4 ~

To be or not to be . . . censors had the final say

As if the creative process wasn't difficult enough, playwrights in Shake-speare's day had to walk a fine line between freely exercising their muses and satisfying city, court, and church authorities. You couldn't put just any old play out on the stage for public consumption. Beginning in 1581, it first had to past muster with the powerful Master of Revels.

In the early days of public performance, censorship was largely self-imposed. To survive, acting companies needed patrons, and it would have been professional suicide for a company to perform material that would have jeopardized the delicate relationship with the man whose name lent legitimacy to their efforts. However, as plays became increasingly popu-lar, London city officials and Puritan leaders began to worry that self-censorship might not be enough. Local authorities feared theaters would become rallying places for the disaffected; they foresaw organized pro-test and riots. Protestant clergy, on the other hand, were convinced that plays had a negative impact on the populace's moral purity. They even claimed plays offered instruction in lying, cheating, stealing, and deceit. Both groups diligently looked for ways to shut the whole thing down. Fortunately, for struggling playwrights and actors at least, Queen Eliza-beth intervened to take control of the playhouses away from city and church officials and to bring it within the purview of the royal court.

According to the proclamation she issued in 1581, official approval of dramatic works was placed in the hands of one Edmund Tilney, who carried the title Master of Revels. Henceforth, it would be his job to peruse every script for passages related to religious or political issues as well as for material that might offend foreign allies or appear to lampoon important people and policies. With regard to individual works, Tilney had three choices: He could pass a play without change, he could demand specific alterations be made to the script, or he could ban the work altogether. In any case, no play could be performed until it had undergone his scrutiny and received his official stamp of approval. And as tempting as it might have been to perform a dramatic work without first clearing it through the Office of Revels, any acting company that hoped to survive would know better. The Master of Revels also had the power to decide which companies could appear before the Queen.

Given the number of his plays performed onstage beginning around 1590 or so, William Shakespeare apparently had little trouble getting past the watchful eyes of Edmund Tilney. There is, however, at least one indication of when he might have had to change a script to satisfy the censors. Raising sensitive issues was apparently another no-no on Tilney's list. One such issue during the reign of Elizabeth I would surely have been the whole matter of abdication. In 1595, when Shakespeare probably wrote *Richard II*, the Queen was childless and rapidly aging, and abdication was a subject never to be discussed. This may explain why the abdication scene Shakespeare originally wrote into his script for *Richard*

II did not appear in printed editions published during Queen Elizabeth's lifetime. It's unlikely that the scene was performed onstage during her reign, either. However, after her death and the ascension of James I, when concerns about abdication were no longer relevant, the scene mysteriously reappeared in printed editions of the play. Did Shakespeare bow to the will of a censor and temporarily strike it out?

41

A changing of the guard

Near the midway point in Shakespeare's playwriting career, the English government underwent an administration change. In 1603, James VI of Scotland came to the English throne as James I, thus launching a period in British history known as the Jacobean era. The arrival of this Scottish king at Whitehall would turn out to be more than a simple switching of the royal guard.

While Elizabeth took her regal duties quite seriously, James appears to have been more bent on enjoying the high life. He and his Danish-born queen, Anne, were the epitome of what we would today call "party animals." Their extravagant lifestyles and lavish parties alienated both Parliament and the heavily taxed public, who bore the brunt of the bills.

James's apparent penchant for handsome young men, whom he some-times elevated to powerful positions, didn't help his public image, either. His son, Charles I, would apparently inherit the same contempt for Parliament and ultimately lose his head as a result.

This is not to say that James I didn't have some good points. He did make peace with Spain, and he managed to keep England out of Europe's Thirty Years War. He continued Elizabeth's course of relative religious tolerance, except when repression was absolutely necessary, as after the Guy Fawkes Catholic rebellion in 1605. But he is most remembered for the accomplishment that bears his name. Early in his reign, James I personally assembled a team of forty-seven scholars for the sole purpose of developing a new and improved translation of the Bible. The resulting King James Bible was published in 1611 and went on to become the English-language standard for Christendom's most important book over the course of the next three centuries. Revered for its lyrical language, the KJV Bible can still be found in many pulpits throughout the world.

For Shakespeare, the ascension of James I would prove a career booster. King James seems to have enjoyed the theater even more than Elizabeth, and he must have liked Shakespeare's acting company in particular. Under James, the company performed before the court some 177 times, compared to only thirty-two royal performances in Queen Elizabeth's day. In fact, King James enjoyed the work of these actors so much, he granted the company his royal patronage. By order of James I, the

Lord Chamberlain's Men officially became "the King's Men" (not the ones who went on to record the hit single "Louie, Louie"). In addition to appearing at least once a month before the royal court, the King's Men continued to perform almost daily on the Globe Theatre's stage. Considering audiences' seemingly unceasing thirst for new material during these times, playwrights, Shakespeare included, must have found themselves under tremendous pressure to produce.

No wonder the Jacobean period seems to have been an intensely creative time for William Shakespeare. Despite another outbreak of the plague, which closed London theaters for much of 1603, Shakespeare continued to churn out two plays per year. Many of his most famous works, including the tragedies *Othello*, *Macbeth*, and *King Lear*, were apparently written during James I's reign. Shakespeare also penned several works that came to be known as the romances—*Cymbeline*, *The Winter's Tale*, and *The Tempest*—during this period. James I's reign saw Shakespeare's prose come to life on paper for the first time as well. The first-ever collection of his plays, appropriately titled *First Folio*, was released for public consumption in 1623, seven years after the playwright's death and two years before a new king, Charles I, would assume the British throne.

⁓42⁓

Nothing new under the sun

Here's a startling thought: Shakespeare didn't invent most of his plots. He copied them from someone else. Whoa . . . wait a minute. Shakespeare copied from other writers? Isn't that illegal?

Not in Elizabethan times it wasn't.

In Shakespeare's day, writing was a free-for-all. As noted in Number 10, there were no laws concerning copyrights and no penalties for plagiarism. Creative works were up for grabs. Lift a line from here, pick a plot from there. No crime. No credit. And no remorse. Everybody does it, so it's perfectly okay.

Considering the pedestal we've put Shakespeare on, it may hurt to think he wasn't above helping himself to someone else's idea. But Renaissance men truly believed imitation to be the sincerest form of flattery; Shakespeare was just carrying on the tradition. To take another playwright's plot and put your unique twist on it would have been considered the noble thing to do.

The pressure to produce may have been partly to blame for this frenzy of imitation among Elizabethan dramatists. To satisfy audience demands for new and better plays, writers had to keep a steady stream of copy coming. There simply wouldn't have been time to spend weeks brainstorming for new ideas. In fact, similarities identified in some works by Marlowe and Shakespeare have led a few scholars to believe that one of the two might have been leaning a little too heavily on the other.

This is not to say that William Shakespeare copied lines from the works of others, then passed them off as his own. That would have been tacky and patently unnecessary, considering his apparent gift for lyrical language and clever wordplay. He did, however, borrow ideas quite liberally from earlier texts, including history books, legends, and classical works of drama, poetry, and prose. The description of Cleopatra on her royal barge in *Antony and Cleopatra*, for example, reads suspiciously like Sir Thomas North's translation of Plutarch, which Shakespeare might well have studied in grammar school. *Hamlet* takes its story from an Old Norse folktale about a prince who faked madness to get revenge. And for *King Lear,* the author drew primarily from a contemporary play titled *The Chronicle History of King Leir* and Holinshed's *Chronicles*. Of course, Shakespeare had his own take on what happened to the king. He added a subplot, also adapted (in this case, from Sir Philip Sidney's *Arcadia*), and turned the previously happy ending into a tragic finale.

~ 43 ~

Building on a great tradition

It's tempting sometimes to think that playacting in England began with William Shakespeare. In truth, a long line of dramatic productions had preceded his entrance on the scene, making it possible for him to do what he did. While it's true that the playhouse tradition in London was barely ten years old when Shakespeare arrived there in 1587, the origins of English popular drama could be traced back many generations.

Long before Will was even a twinkle in his father's eye, people in England were putting on plays. At first they were simple religious pageants made up of chants and prayers performed by priests on the steps of cathedrals. Later, familiar Bible stories were embellished to create simple plays centering on popular Old Testament characters such as Noah, Abraham, Moses, and David. In the late fourteenth century, religious drama became a more formal mode of entertainment with the introduction of the so-called mystery or Corpus Christi plays. Performed at outdoor festivals by traveling troupes of amateur actors throughout the spring and summer, these plays—a complete cycle meant to depict the entire history of the world—dramatized Biblical events from Creation to the Last Judgment, with special emphasis on the life of Christ.

The morality plays, which came next, could easily be considered the direct forerunners of Elizabethan drama. These productions, pitting vice against virtue, were allegories meant to teach a moral lesson. The play's protagonist would likely be called Everyman and the opponents he had to face down or embrace might be named after such qualities as Mercy, Kindness, Greed, or Envy. The battle to overcome temptation onstage would be a fierce one for Everyman, but virtue would always prevail.

It was but a small step from morality plays to popular drama. Shakespeare's early histories, for example, were essentially struggles between good and evil. The audiences for these plays would have been able to readily identify the lesson about human behavior depicted onstage. At the same time that morality plays were evolving into what would come to be known as the Elizabethan dramatic style, classical Greek and Latin literature was undergoing a revival. Lessons learned in the Latin grammar schools provided up-and-coming English playwrights with plenty of engaging story lines for their new plays. Shakespeare is known to have pulled heavily from works by Plutarch, Ovid, and other classical writers for his plots, a perfectly acceptable practice in an age when copyrights were unheard of and plagiarism was not considered a crime.

Of course, truly creative people wouldn't have been content to simply copy from the works of others and, in this regard, Shakespeare was no exception. He put his own distinctive twists on the classics to come up with many memorable characters and quotable lines that were uniquely his own. So the next time you go to the theater to see a modern production, remember to thank Shakespeare. He and his contemporaries invented many of the plot devices we still see onstage. And just as Elizabethan drama evolved from its predecessors, today's Broadway productions may be directly traced to the plays that audiences were enjoying more than 400 years ago.

~44~
At last, a place to call home

The year 1576 marked a pivotal point in the history of British theater. That year, James Burbage, a carpenter turned manager of the acting company the Earl of Leicester's Men, built a playhouse on a piece of land he had leased in Shoreditch, just north of the London city limits. Until then, his traveling troupe of actors had performed wherever they were welcome—in farm fields, open-air marketplaces, courtyards, and inns. Now this itinerant group had a permanent place to call home.

Burbage aptly dubbed his brand-new playhouse the Theatre. It would be the first such structure in London, but it certainly wouldn't be the last. Whether he intended to or not, Burbage had launched a movement. Within a year, a second theater, the Curtain, had opened its doors across the street. Not to be outdone, Burbage's chief financial rival, Philip Henslowe, put up a playhouse in 1587 for his company, the Lord Admiral's Men, which he called the Rose. But instead of locating his new theater near the other two playhouses north of London, Henslowe built in a neighborhood known as Bankside, on the south side of the Thames. The Rose proved wildly successful thanks to the reputation of the Lord Admiral's Men, who made it their home, and the work of resident playwrights such as Christopher Marlowe and Thomas Kyd.

Francis Langley, a goldsmith who must have thought he'd found the way to make an easy pound or two, put up the next playhouse on the south side of the Thames in 1595; he named it the Swan. Unfortunately, this venture would prove a disaster. Built without a resident company, the Swan had a tough time competing with productions staged by the Lord Admiral's Men at the Rose and the Lord Chamberlain's Men, who by now had taken over Burbage's Theatre. The final blow for the Swan came in 1597, when the Office of Revels shut it down following a production of Thomas Nashe's *The Isle of Dogs*, a play considered to be seditious.

When James Burbage died in 1597, he left the Theatre to his sons, Cuthbert and Richard. Within two years, they lost the land lease. Rather than lose the building, too, Richard and his players dismantled the structure in the dead of night and sneaked the timbers across the frozen Thames to Bankside, where they reassembled the building within a few months and christened it the Globe (see Number 51). William Shakespeare, by this time a successful playwright, would join the Burbage brothers, along with several actors, as a shareholder in the Globe's resident acting company, the Lord Chamberlain's Men (later the King's Men). Over the next few years, many of his most famous plays would be staged here.

By 1600, the Globe had become *the* place to go in London for quality drama. The new theater was so successful it threatened to put the Rose right out of business. In response, Philip Henslowe moved his Lord Admiral's Men to the other side of the Thames, near where the great theater wars had begun in the first place. He built the Fortune north of London, in Finsbury, on a piece of land his son-in-law, the actor Edward Alleyn, had acquired in 1599. Henslowe didn't entirely abandon the Bankside theater district, however. In 1613, he turned an old bear-baiting arena on the south side of the Thames into the Hope, a multipurpose venue for animal fights and dramatic productions.

That same year, unfortunately, would spell an end for the Globe. During a performance of Shakespeare's *Henry VIII*, a spark from one of the stage cannons ignited the thatch roof and the playhouse burned to the ground. The King's Men subsequently took up residence at the Blackfriars theater, another Burbage-owned property. Blackfriars was an indoor theater, offering highbrow productions aimed primarily at the nobility. Some of Shakespeare's later plays, including *The Tempest* and *The Winter's Tale*, may have been written specifically for Blackfriars, where the setting was more intimate and the audience might have been more sophisticated.

~45~
The company you kept

Modern-day actors can easily command six-figure salaries and more. Their Elizabethan counterparts, even the ones with star power, wouldn't have come close. In the ladder of social success, actors in Shakespeare's time were considered one rung above vagrants and beggars.

If you wanted to become rich, acting was clearly not the way to go. But if you were determined to act and you wanted to survive, aligning yourself with a company of actors was something you had to do. With membership in a company came not only the camaraderie of other players, but also protection in the form of a highly placed patron. For the most part, patrons did little more than lend their names to the acting troupe, but that could be helpful. Should some person in authority threaten to make trouble for an individual actor or even close an entire production down, a little creative name-dropping could often save the day. Because wages depended on the number of tickets sold, it behooved an aspiring actor to align himself with a popular company. If you were good enough, you might work your way up from nonacting jobs to bit parts to leading roles, and eventually you might even become a shareholder in the company's profits.

In Shakespeare's day, the leading theater companies were the Lord Admiral's Men and the Lord Chamberlain's Men (later the King's Men).

Shakespeare belonged to the latter from 1594 until he returned to Stratford around 1613. Theater companies varied in size, with the Lord Chamberlain's Men being one of the largest. Typically, an acting company would have a membership of about twelve to sixteen regular players; temporary extras would be hired as needed. Since plays could have twenty-five or thirty parts, actors performed multiple roles in a single play.

Theater companies were organized in a three-tiered hierarchy. At the top were the sharers—the leading players who invested money in the company, then shared in its profits or losses. Playwrights were usually not sharers; Shakespeare was the exception. He owned a share of the Lord Chamberlain's Men, and presumably this is how he made the bulk of his money. An individual player's share was determined by the amount he invested in the enterprise up front. Companies with favorite actors and popular productions could generate substantial earnings for shareholders.

Next in line were the hired men, paid weekly wages. This group included actors in minor roles, musicians, wardrobe keepers, stagehands, and the vitally important book-holder, who acted as a combination script-minder, stage manager, and prompter. The book-holder was responsible for keeping track of the court-approved script (also called a "prompt-book") at all times and for noting any changes made during rehearsals. At the bottom of the heap were the apprentices, who played the roles of children and women. They were paid next to nothing; room and board, plus the training they received from the experienced players who served as their mentors, would have been considered compensation enough.

46

Star power

Elizabethan theater was, in some ways, not so different from our own. Audiences didn't line up for play tickets because they liked the writer. They went to see their favorite stars. Just as modern-day audiences are drawn to headliners like Brad Pitt, Mel Gibson, and Tom Cruise, Elizabethans flocked to see Edward Alleyn, Richard Burbage, and Will Kempe.

In the 1580s, just before Shakespeare arrived on the scene, the Lord Admiral's Men ranked as the leading acting company in London. The aristocratic Philip Henslowe served as its flamboyant manager; his son-in-law Edward Alleyn was the company's principal actor and perhaps the first bona fide superstar of the London stage. At well over six feet tall, Alleyn's commanding presence and his deep, rich voice (tailor-made for the soliloquies so popular in Elizabethan drama) drew legions of fans. A particular favorite of Christopher Marlowe, Alleyn starred in the original productions of *Dr. Faustus* and *Tamburlaine the Great*.

By the late 1590s, however, Alleyn's star was beginning to wane. The author of his best roles (Marlowe) was dead, and the upstart Lord Chamberlain's Men had begun its bid to take the top spot among London-based acting companies. Everyone who wanted to be someone in the London theater world, including aspiring stars of the stage and rising young playwrights such as William Shakespeare, scurried to ally themselves with the Lord Chamberlain's Men. These enterprising thespians would become so successful that they would oust the Lord Admiral's Men as the number-one acting company and earn royal patronage under James I, making them the King's Men.

The leading dramatic actor in this up-and-coming company of players was Richard Burbage. In 1576, his father James, also an actor, had built the Theatre, the first public playhouse in London. From all indications, Richard Burbage was an especially convincing player. He became a favorite among Elizabethan audiences, eventually usurping Alleyn's dominance, with his realistic portrayals of tragic heroes. In all likelihood, Shakespeare wrote the characters of Hamlet, Othello, and King Lear expressly for Richard Burbage.

Another of the stars allied with the Lord Chamberlain's Men was Will Kempe. The leading comedic actor of his day, Kempe relied more on physical stunts and verbal confusion than wit for laughs. His jigs and comic dances were particularly popular with audiences. Although playbills from the period do not survive, it is probably safe to assume that Kempe originated the roles of Bottom and Falstaff. He almost certainly played Peter in *Romeo and Juliet* and Dogberry in *Much Ado About Nothing*. Kempe left the company in 1599 for reasons that are unclear. Perhaps he was simply tired of the day-to-day acting grind. What we do know, however, is that he did not go quietly. As a final exit and publicity stunt, Kempe danced his way from London to Norwich, a distance of more than 100 miles, in just nine days.

Kempe's successor in Shakespeare's comedic roles was Robert Armin, whose style was more that of the tragic clown. He often played the fool who gets away with mocking his superiors and raising questions about authority. For Armin, Shakespeare created such roles as Feste in *Twelfth Night* and the Fool in *King Lear*.

~47~
It wasn't Broadway, baby

Attendance at a Shakespearean production in the twenty-first century is largely a passive experience. You take your seat in front of a stage, you wait for the curtain to rise, and, except for an occasional outburst of applause, you generally sit quietly in the semidarkness and simply let the players do their work. If you like the play, you may clap enthusiastically at the final curtain and call for an encore. If you don't, you'll either leave between acts or simply wait it out politely in silence, then go home and tell your friends.

Not so in Elizabethan England.

Going to the theater in Shakespeare's day was an interactive encounter. As a member of the audience, you would have been expected to participate in the action. Elizabethan theaters featured a stage standing approximately three to five feet off the ground and extending out into the audience, which surrounded it on three sides. There were no curtains and little or no scenery. Elaborate costumes had a twofold purpose: They helped create the dramatic illusion, and they separated the men from the boys, who played the female parts. They may or may not have been authentic to the play's supposed time and place. Elizabethan audiences were not picky about such things.

Theaters were not designed with any uniform plan or size in mind; some may have accommodated as many as 2,500 to 3,500 people. Unlike modern theaters, where the cheapest seats are the farthest from the stage, Elizabethan theaters had a rather sizable section reserved directly in front of the players for the so-called groundlings—the common laborers, artisans, and prostitutes who frequented the theater district. These theatergoers would have probably paid about a penny—the equivalent of a day's wage in those times—for standing-room-only "seats" and they would have expected a good value for their money.

Given the proximity of the audience to the stage, the actors couldn't help but deliver their lines directly to the crowd, and the crowd, in turn, couldn't resist answering back. If they liked a particular performance, they might shout some encouragement or clap loudly. If they didn't, they made their disdain known with hoots, hollers, boos, and the not-so-occasional missile in the form of an orange.

Acting companies had to be on their toes because competition for public attention would have been stiff in those days. Unlike Broadway, where a single production may run for many years, the playbill at an Elizabethan theater changed frequently. Also, there were several theaters, not to mention other forms of entertainment. If you didn't fancy the theater, you could witness a public execution, by hanging, beheading, or any number of other gruesome ways. You just never knew who was going to die, or which of the victims might be tarred and feathered, drawn and quartered, or simply butchered. Baiting was another popular spectator sport. Packs of dogs or bulls and bears would be turned loose to battle one another to the death. And then there was the ever-popular "pike-pitching." Following beheadings, the heads of traitors were left to rot on pikes, and passersby made a game out of flinging rotten fruit and animal dung at the remains. Kind of makes you wonder about the phrase "the good old days," doesn't it?

~48~

A playwright for the people

We tend to think of a Shakespeare production as pretty highbrow stuff, but that wouldn't have been the case in the playwright's own time. Believe it or not, William Shakespeare wrote for the common man and woman.

Who went to see a Shakespearean play? Just about anyone and everyone. Reports from the period suggest that roughly 13 percent of the total London population in those days regularly attended the theater. At their peak, London's playhouses attracted a combined total of 8,000 to 10,000 people per day. These numbers suggest that Elizabethan audiences must have come from all walks of life.

Most theaters in those days were open-air, and playgoers came to be seen as much as they came to see. Performances at public playhouses took place in the daylight, which meant that members of the audience could get a good look at one another. If you hoped to attract the attention of the opposite sex, which many did, you wanted to look your best. Unfortunately for the players, an audience never sat quietly for long. They might call out to one another across the gallery, eat, drink, and smoke their clay pipes. But when a trumpet blared, they knew something important was about to happen so they turned their full attention to the action onstage. And they were always prepared to be enchanted.

Just like a good mystery or romance novel today, Shakespeare's plays would have provided escape from an otherwise humdrum existence. True, some of his plots were far-fetched, but that's exactly what an Elizabethan audience would have demanded. They loved fantasies about witches and fairies, tales of impossible love affairs, and improbable plans for revenge. They went to the theater not to relive the grim details of their own lives, but to forget them by spending a few hours in a make-believe world.

Shakespeare wrote something to appeal to all levels of sophistication and intelligence. His more philosophical passages would have been aimed at the nobility; low comedy, like the kind the actor Will Kempe excelled at, would have delighted the groundlings. And of course there was plenty of sex and violence for all.

And while we struggle with the intricacies of Shakespeare's convoluted plots and complicated dialogue, Elizabethans would probably have easily understood it all. They were excellent audiences because they were adept at listening. The majority of them didn't know how to read. They would have been used to relying completely on their sense of hearing to comprehend literary works, which would have made it much easier for them to pick up on the nuances of Shakespeare's words.

Once bitten by the theater bug, Elizabethans seem to have had an insatiable appetite for dramatic productions. Playwrights and actors churned out a never-ending stream of new material to meet the growing demand. Surely no Broadway dramatist today could be expected to keep up such a furious pace as the one Will Shakespeare likely endured.

~49~

Psst . . . Juliet was really a guy

Shakespeare's *Romeo and Juliet* has long reigned as one of the most romantic love stories of all time. Who can forget that heart-wrenching question, "Oh Romeo, Romeo! wherefore art thou Romeo?" It came from the lips of sweet Juliet, who in the original production—sit down for this one— would have been a man.

That's right. Shakespeare's Juliet was really a guy. So were Ophelia, Desdemona, Miranda, Lady Macbeth, and even Cleopatra. Shakespeare wrote about mothers, daughters, girlfriends, and wives. But no matter which name they went by or how varied their personalities and motivations, Shakespeare's ladies shared one thing in common: Onstage, they were all young men or boys.

In Elizabethan times, women were not allowed to perform onstage. Preteen and teenage boys, whose figures were slight enough to pass for feminine and whose voices had not yet changed, took the female parts. No matter that when Romeo kissed Juliet, two men were locking lips. Playgoers were willing to accept the illusion, even when it took an unusual turn, which Shakespeare delighted in providing.

Consider, for example, the case of Olivia in *Twelfth Night*, who falls in love with Cesario, who is actually Viola disguised as a male page in order to win favor with Duke Orsino. If you find this scenario confusing, imagine how complicated it must have been for an Elizabethan theatergoer, who would have seen a boy dressed as a girl in love with a boy dressed as a girl dressed as a boy. Huh?

That males portrayed females in Shakespeare's plays is hardly surprising. Greek and Latin classical drama were male-only traditions. So was (still is) Kabuki in Japan. Then, too, there was the matter of women's roles in the daily life of Elizabethan England. Disregard the fact that a woman—Elizabeth I—was head of state. As explained in Number 38, ordinary women were second-class citizens, raised to be wives and mothers, nothing more. A girl was considered lucky if she attended grammar school; a university education would have been out of the question.

Women in Shakespeare's time were subservient to men, charged with keeping house and keeping quiet. They gathered the eggs, milked the cows, baked the bread, churned the butter, swept the floors, and, oh yes, bore and reared a brood of children. And while some women did learn how to read, few bothered to write. What was the point? Their words would hardly have been deemed important enough to save. As for acting, well, that wasn't given so much as a thought. Women had more "important" things to do.

Across the channel, however, women performed frequently onstage, so it was only a matter of time before male domination of the English theater ended. In 1662 King Charles II licensed women to act on the English stage, and in 1676 Margaret Hughes became the first to join a company that performed Shakespeare. Dozens of English actresses followed in her wake.

Yet even after women began regularly appearing in Shakespeare's plays, skeptics remained. "Alas," these die-hard fans of boy actors insisted, "no woman can play Juliet so well."

~*5*°~

No such thing as stunt men

If you wanted to be an actor in Shakespeare's day, you had to do more than memorize your lines and project them loudly enough to outshout a rowdy audience, who didn't hesitate to let you know what they thought of your performance. Depending on the play and the part, you might also have to sing, dance, juggle, wield a sword, throw a knife or an axe, and maybe perform magic tricks. Elizabethan acting companies didn't have specially trained personnel to handle the stunts. It was up to the actor to pull the whole thing off. And that was no easy feat.

Typically, the stage in an Elizabethan theater extended out into the audience, giving playgoers a bird's-eye view of the action. There was no way you could fake it. And since this was live theater, there were no retakes, either. Mess up on a stunt the first time around and you'd probably get booed off the stage. Your audience had paid good money for their tickets—maybe even given up the chance to witness a public execution down the street. They expected quality entertainment. If a sword fight was meant to be thrilling, it better look that way. No half-hearted thrusts or clumsy lunges allowed. You had to make it as close to the real thing as you could without hurting your opponent.

Stages in those days were bare-bones affairs. There was no curtain to raise at the opening of a play; the action was usually launched by a single player who stepped onstage to set the scene with a few lines of dialogue, or chorus. Players usually made entrances and exits through two doorways, which led to the "tiring house" (short for attiring house, what we'd call a dressing room) backstage.

Elaborate costumes made up for the lack of scenery, but they weren't always accurate to time period or setting. Elizabethan audiences didn't seem to care about accuracy, as long as the costumes were fun to look at. Regardless of whether the action was supposed to be taking place in England, Egypt, or Italy, in the current century or several before, they knew the play's message was meant to apply directly to them. The appropriateness of the clothing didn't matter a whit.

Battle scenes were particularly vivid. Audiences expected that a skirmish onstage meant the clashing of swords and the firing of real cannons. Trumpets were often used to announce the beginning of a battle or to signal the entrance of a key character. Jigs and clowning were regular features, too, even in tragedies like *King Lear*.

There were no fades to black to signal a scene change or to conceal the movement of props. When a character "died" onstage, he would be carried off with a dramatic flourish; there was no other way to get rid of him. Certain intense actions, like the murder of Desdemona in *Othello* or that famous after-dark meeting between Romeo and Juliet, might take place in an alcove set off to one side of the stage or on a balcony specially constructed in the back wall. A trapdoor in the stage floor was often used to simulate a ghost rising out of the grave.

For the most part, special effects worked, but on occasion, they could go horribly awry. Perhaps the most devastating example of a stunt gone wrong occurred in 1613, when a spark from one of the stage cannons ignited the thatched roof of the Globe (see Number 51).

⟨*51*⟩

Going Global

The Globe Theatre would make an interesting story even if you didn't know about its connection with Shakespeare. The details surrounding the birth and death of this celebrated playhouse represent the stuff from which legends are made.

The Globe came into the world one winter night in 1598 thanks to equal measures of grit and chutzpah. A year before, the Burbage boys—Cuthbert and Richard—had inherited their father's famous playhouse, the Theatre, in Shoreditch (see Number 44). Somehow, whether through mismanagement or just plain bad luck, the sons lost the Theatre's land lease. The building itself, they heard, was slated for demolition, and rather than risk that, too, they concocted a daring scheme. Richard enlisted a carpenter and several of his actor friends to dismantle the Theatre in the dead of the night, then carry the timbers across the frozen Thames to

Bankside, which had become London's thriving theater district. There, over the course of the next few months, they assembled a new building from those timbers. When the work was finished eight months later, the Burbages christened their new creation the Globe.

Built by actors for actors, the Globe was, in its day, the finest theater London had ever seen. Polygonal (twenty-four sides) in shape, it featured a massive stage and three tiers of galleries for the audience. Reports from the period indicate it may have accommodated as many as 2,000 spectators in seats and another 800 groundlings, who would have stood in front of and around three sides of the stage. A thatched roof protected the playgoers who could afford to fork out as much as a shilling for the most expensive seats; those in the pit, who paid about a penny for their spots, stood directly beneath the blazing sun or chilly drizzle.

From the beginning, William Shakespeare was the Globe's resident playwright and a shareholder in the company of actors—the Lord Chamberlain's Men (later the King's Men)—that performed there. Many of his later works, including *Julius Caesar*, *As You Like It*, *Hamlet*, *Macbeth*, and *King Lear* would likely have made their debuts on this stage; his last play, *Henry VIII*, written in collaboration with John Fletcher, brought down the house. Literally.

While the birth of the Globe—which began with the dismantling of the Theatre—took place under cover of darkness, the death of the Globe was anything but secretive. The original Globe Theatre went out in a true blaze of glory. On July 29, 1613, during a performance of *Henry VIII*, a spark from one of the cannons shot off to signal the entrance of the king caught the thatched roof on fire. The audience was apparently so caught up in the action onstage that no one noticed the smoke. By the time they did, the building was beyond saving.

It was not, however, beyond reconstructing—twice. A second Globe Theatre was built on the same site a few years later. It was demolished, along with the rest of London's Elizabethan theaters, around 1644, following the Puritan Revolution. However, a third Globe Theatre, reconstructed in the mid-1990s to replicate the original, now offers regular performances of Shakespeare's plays in a period setting.

PART III

The Language

Familiar in their mouths
as household words . . .
—KING HENRY V

MAKING SENSE OF SHAKESPEARE'S LANGUAGE

REMEMBER the last time you said *prithee*, *mayhap*, or *perchance*? Would you describe yourself as a clotpole? A flibbertigibbet? A slug-a-bed? Could you define and conjugate the verbs *slubber*, *shog*, or *thwack*? Probably not. All of these terms—household words in Shakespeare's time—are long gone from our lexicon. No wonder the mere thought of reading one of Shakespeare's plays strikes fear in many a student's heart. The man wasn't even speaking English, for crying out loud!

Literary scholars agree that William Shakespeare had a wonderful way with words. But to appreciate his work fully, you have to know a little something about the state of the English language at the time he wrote and how he shaped it to suit his purposes. His choice of words and phrasing served not only to advance his plots and create enduring images, but also to provide us with windows into the souls of characters we'll never forget.

~52~

Before there was Shakespeare

The English language has come a long way, baby, and most of its evolution took place long before Shakespeare arrived on the scene. Believe it or not, the language he spoke and wrote was remarkably like our own. Its roots can be traced to Anglo-Saxon, a Germanic-based language that superseded the existing Celtic tongue in Britain after Angles, Saxons, and Jutes from Denmark and Germany overran the natives and settled there. As a separate language, Anglo-Saxon didn't last long. In terms of the spoken word, borders can be quite porous, and even in an island kingdom like Britain, language has a way of not remaining untouched. Pure Anglo-Saxon has all but disappeared, but if you want to take a stab at deciphering some, try reading *Beowulf.*

William the Conqueror was the first to water down the Anglo-Saxon tongue. When he crossed the channel to invade the British Isles in 1066, he brought more than weapons and warriors; he brought another language. In the decades following the battle of Hastings, the new rulers of England spoke Norman French, and before long their words permeated pure Anglo-Saxon. Meanwhile, in continental Europe, Latin remained the language of choice for the educated classes and was widely used in the practice of law, medicine, commerce, and religion. Latin soon infiltrated the Germanic-based Anglo-Saxon. Thus, by about 1400, the residents of England were speaking to one another in a language that combined French, Latin, and Anglo-Saxon words. This new tongue, known as Middle English, is the practically indecipherable one modern students struggle with when they try to read Chaucer's *Canterbury Tales*.

By the time Shakespeare began writing, less than 200 years later, Middle English had evolved into a form that, with careful reading, we can easily understand today. The language of Shakespeare's time became known as Early Modern English. Its gradual evolution into Later Modern English, around the middle of the seventeenth century, takes us pretty close to the language spoken in twenty-first-century America.

Confused? Don't be. Even in their original form, Shakespeare's plays are easier to decipher than *The Canterbury Tales*. Although many of the words Shakespeare used have disappeared and some have changed their meanings, you'll still find familiar terms. Shakespeare was a master at coining the clever turn of phrase. He probably did more than almost any other writer before or since to make our native language colorful and descriptive. Many words we use today, such as *ill-tempered*, *eyesore*, *laughingstock*, and *cold-blooded*, are words Shakespeare invented. Etymologists—the people who study words and their origins—estimate that Shakespeare used approximately 25,000 different words in his plays. Of those, Shakespeare either first recorded or originated 2,000 of them.

Shakespeare would have had to pull all 25,000 of those words out of his head. The first authoritative English-language dictionary, Samuel Johnson's *A Dictionary of the English Language*, was published in 1755.

~53~
Taking Shakespeare out of context

If Shakespeare's work is difficult to understand, perhaps it's because we're trying too hard to take his language out of context. The brand of English he spoke and wrote was still a far cry from our own. If we're confused by Elizabethan verbs like *slubber* (to be careless or messy) or *twire* (to peep), just imagine how Will Shakespeare would feel if he were dropped into the twenty-first century and had to cope with some of ours. What would he make of the following sentence: "I think I'll prioritize my to-do list while I nuke a burrito for dinner?"

Many of the words Shakespeare used have disappeared from our English vocabulary, and the Elizabethan definitions for others have long since disappeared. When Shakespeare describes someone as *roynish* or *orgulous*, he might as well be speaking a foreign tongue. Webster's latest collegiate edition doesn't tell us that the first meant "coarse" and the second "haughty"; it doesn't include them at all. Nor does it offer "diffident" as a definition for *nice* or "foolish" as a synonym for *fond*; Shakespeare and his audience would have understood both and used the words accordingly.

The English language was still evolving in Shakespeare's time, and he may have found the whole thing a bit confusing himself, particularly as it relates to verb forms. Perhaps that's why, within the same play, and sometimes even out of the same character's mouth, you're likely to hear both *do* and *doth*, *has* and *hath*, *go* and *goeth*. Shakespeare isn't much clearer on exactly when to use formal and informal personal pronouns, either. To our ears, the word *thou* sounds pretty stilted, but to Elizabethans it was an informal version of *you*—much like the Spanish *tú* or German *du*—reserved for use only between family and friends. By virtue of his position, a king could call anyone *thou*, but only his immediate family could return the favor, and only in private. In *Richard III*, the king addresses Tyrrel as *thou*; Tyrrel, in turn, correctly refers to the king as *you* or *my lord*. In *King Lear*, on the other hand, the Fool addresses Lear as *thou*, a blatant social faux pas if ever there was one. In this case, Shakespeare's misuse was consistent with the Fool's overall behavior to his "master."

To make sense of Shakespeare's language, you have to put yourself in an ordinary Elizabethan's shoes. He or she would have understood the playwright's references to classical mythology, falconry, and astrology—all three were well known in those days. That peculiar notion about human behavior called the theory of humors would also have helped Elizabethans appreciate character motivation in Shakespeare's time. (See Number 36 for more on the four humors.) When Hamlet turned melancholy and started all that introspective musing, we'd figure it was a bout of depression brought on by years spent coping with a dysfunctional family. Your average Elizabethan would have known it was nothing more than an overabundance of black bile. One measure of Shakespeare's greatness is that we'd be as right as the Elizabethans were.

~54~
Words were his currency

If ever a writer epitomized the phrase "He had a way with words," the leading candidate would be William Shakespeare. Never before or since has a single writer had such an impact on our language. He had a natural gift for putting words on paper. What he lacked in formal education, he more than made up for in raw talent.

It's obvious that Shakespeare delighted in words. He played with them as if he were a child and they were his toys—adding a prefix here, tacking on a suffix there, stringing a pair of nouns together with a hyphen to create the perfect descriptor. In Shakespeare's world, suns did not set, they *bedimmed*; armies *enrounded* their enemies; and rascals could be downright *traitorly*. Like most Elizabethans, Shakespeare loved puns, and he worked them into his plays whenever possible. *Love's Labor's Lost* contains an estimated 200 puns; the average per play was around eighty. Many of Shakespeare's original puns depended on words that were spelled differently but sounded alike. This can sometimes pose a problem for modern audiences. Unless properly executed onstage, puns such as these are lost because new pronunciations of the words have made them moot. (Perhaps that explains why *Love's Labor's Lost* is not one of Shakespeare's more popular plays.) Still, we can appreciate lines such as "Your means are very slender, and your waste is great" when they are directed at memorable characters such as the portly Falstaff.

Like most writers, Shakespeare would have almost certainly ago-
nized over his language. When he couldn't find the perfect word, he
simply invented one. As noted in Number 52, of the estimated 25,000
different words found in his plays, approximately 2,000 were brand-new;
Shakespeare either recorded them for the first time or originated them.
The next time you feel the urge to puke, thank William Shakespeare for
giving you that word, along with *bandit, critic, gossip, jig, numb, obscene,
kissing, quarrelsome*, and *torture*, to name a few. Oh, and by the way, that
rumor going around that Shakespeare coined the term *gadzooks*? It's just
not true. *Logger-headed, pestiferous, zounds, thwack*, and *slug-a-bed*, yes.
But *gadzooks*? Nope, that wasn't Shakespeare.

One out of about every twelve words Shakespeare used was a new one
that appeared only once throughout his entire body of work. Whether
this was by accident or design, no one knows, or if they do, they're not
talking. Maybe they're just worn out from accounting for all 25,000 different words. After all, the King James Bible, another work from the
same era as Shakespeare, only had 6,000 dissimilar words. And just in
case you wake up some morning around 3 A.M. and can't go back to sleep
until you know exactly where in Shakespeare to find *clotpole, lubberly,*
or *swoopstake*, there is relief for your language-induced insomnia. *The
Harvard Concordance to Shakespeare* reputedly lists, in alphabetical order,
every word he ever wrote and where to find it.

To save you a trip to the bookstore for your own personal copy, we'll go ahead and tell you that his longest word—*honorificabilitudinitatibus*—appears in *Love's Labor's Lost*. Loosely translated, it means having an overabundance of honorableness, but the character who utters it is mainly using it as an example of a long word, as someone might use *antidisestablishmentarianism* today. You get a gold star if you can work it into a casual conversation (you have to pronounce it correctly, of course), two gold stars if you can spell it without looking!

~55~
When poetry ruled the stage

The language of Shakespeare's plays takes two basic forms: poetry and prose. Most plays contain a blend of the two. Which form Shakespeare chose to use depends largely on who's talking and what point the author wishes to make. Poetry tends to catch the ear more quickly than prose, so weighty issues were usually handled in verse. Serious characters with important things to say typically spoke in poetry; comic characters, who were almost always from the lower classes and provided a welcome break from sober subjects, more often spoke in prose.

A good example of a Shakespeare play containing both poetry and prose is *Henry IV, Part I*. Not surprisingly, King Henry speaks in verse, and the comic Falstaff speaks in prose. Prince Hal talks with Falstaff and his other friends in prose, perhaps to indicate that he's just one of the guys. But when he addresses the audience, his words are in blank verse. This change helps the audience to understand just how calculating Hal is in his choice of lifestyle.

Sometimes, instead of mixing poetry and prose in a play, Shakespeare would choose to use only one form or the other. For example, *Richard II* is written almost entirely in verse, whereas *The Merry Wives of Windsor* is mostly prose.

Although modern dramatists rarely write in poetry, this was common in Shakespeare's time. Poetry is easier to memorize, and since Elizabethan actors had to carry several plays and parts in their heads at one time, this would have been a plus. The poetry in Shakespeare's plays is primarily blank (unrhymed) verse; rhymed couplets signify the end of a scene or of a sequence of scenes. In a time when there were no curtains to bring down or stage lights to dim, the rhymed lines would have sounded different enough from the rest of the dialogue that the audience would have immediately sensed something onstage was about to change.

As a dramatist, Shakespeare wrote for the ear, so while there's no rhyme in blank verse, there is a definite rhythm to his poetry—iambic pentameter. Typically, a line of his blank verse consists of five two-syllable units (feet) in which the stress falls on the second syllable. Shakespeare was a master at using the rhythm of his words to set a specific mood or tone; his verse could be quickened to create fantasy in one play, slowed down to depict tragic passion in another. But even when he was writing in straight prose, his words still had a magical rhythm. As an actor himself, it's likely that Shakespeare would have read his lines out loud as he wrote them. He would have known when the rhythm worked and when it didn't, and he would have made appropriate adjustments.

Shakespeare's work is often hard for us to comprehend because we're not used to listening to dialogue as poetry. The words sound stilted and stiff. Elizabethan audiences would not have had this problem. Since most of them were illiterate, any learning they did was dependent on the voice and ear. Flowery language and rhymes were common, especially in male-female relationships. If a young man wanted to impress a young lady, he wrote a sonnet (or memorized someone else's) and recited it to her on bended knee. We laugh about that now, but to Elizabethans, poetry was a serious and commonplace form of communication.

~56~
Playing it by ear

Remember the first time an English teacher assigned you the reading of a Shakespearean play? Even before you cracked open the book, you were worried. You just knew Shakespeare was going to be hard . . . full of long-winded characters with names you could barely pronounce, who spoke a peculiar kind of English you'd never get the hang of. You hated Shakespeare's work before you ever even read it.

You were not alone . . . then or now. The thought of studying Shakespeare still strikes fear in the hearts of students everywhere. And the one person who'd be least surprised by that attitude just might be the author himself. Shakespeare meant for his plays to be performed, not read. He wrote for the ear and not the eye. And as any contemporary radio announcer can tell you, there's a major difference.

Although we have no way of knowing exactly how Shakespeare worked, it's probably safe to assume that he spoke his words aloud as he wrote them. His livelihood depended on pleasing an audience and, just like modern-day broadcast advertising copywriters, he would have worked and reworked lines until they sounded just right.

Remember, in Shakespeare's day, it wasn't just the elite who attended the theater. The public playhouses drew all classes: nobles, merchants, artisans, apprentices, and even prostitutes. Since education wasn't available to everyone, a significant share of Shakespeare's audiences would have been illiterate. Even if a printed copy of a playscript had been available in advance of a production, almost no one would have been able to read it. But that doesn't mean they couldn't understand it. The audiences for Shakespeare's plays were illiterate, not stupid. They conducted all of their day-to-day business by speaking and listening, so they had fine-tuned their ears to the nuances of speech. In many ways, they were probably better audiences than we are. They would have understood the jokes and they would have grasped the finer points of Shakespeare's messages.

You can miss a lot by simply reading Shakespeare. On paper, a line meant to be ironic can come across as anything but. Only the actor's inflection onstage can deliver the true intent. For example, Marc Antony calls Brutus "an honorable man" in *Julius Caesar*. On the printed page, the sarcasm in those words may escape a reader; onstage, a good actor will let everyone know what Antony really thinks of Brutus.

If you're having trouble understanding Shakespeare's language, try reading it aloud. Don't let the unfamiliar names and peculiar words stop you. There's a rhythm and a rightness to Shakespeare's work that can only be appreciated when you play it by ear.

~57~
Can right this be?

As difficult as it may seem if you've ever struggled to read one of Shakespeare's plays, the English the author spoke and wrote was pretty close to our own. The fact that we have trouble deciphering it often has more to do with syntax and structure than with the words themselves.

To understand Shakespeare, you have to look first at his sentences' structure. Remember, William Shakespeare was a product of the Latin grammar school system and as such he would have written and spoken the language fluently. If you've ever studied Italian, French, or Spanish, all derived from Latin, you know their sentence structure is very different from English. In Latin, as well as in the modern European Romance languages and pure Anglo-Saxon, the order of words in a sentence is unimportant because of inflection. Words take their meanings from different endings dependent on the role the words play in a given sentence. Nouns have gender and double negatives are status quo. By contrast, modern English is typically uninflected; meanings may vary depending on where certain words appear in a sentence. The typical structure—the one with which we feel most comfortable—is subject-verb-object. In grammatically correct English, objects come after verbs, adjectives usually precede nouns, and prepositions normally precede their objects. And, oh yes, double negatives are a no-no. If these basic precepts are to be considered measures of good writing, then Shakespeare wouldn't have made it past his first modern-day middle-school English class.

Of course in Shakespeare's day, English was still evolving from its Latin, French, and Anglo-Saxon roots, so the concept of uninflected structure as we know it would have been alien to Elizabethan dramatists. Writing was still a free-for-all with no rules about where an object should appear and whether an adjective should go before or after the noun. It's hardly surprising Shakespeare came up with such curious statements as "And left us to the rage of France, his sword" in *Henry VI, Part I*, and had Macbeth pose the backward question to Banquo, "Ride you this afternoon?" And let's not forget double negatives. Celia's exclamation, "I pray you bear with me; I cannot go no further," in *As You Like It* would make any self-respecting twenty-first-century English teacher grit his or her teeth. It all sounded perfectly normal to Shakespeare's audiences.

Like all great writers, Shakespeare created his own unique style. To do that, he occasionally broke whatever grammatical rules might have been in place at the time. He turned verbs into nouns and vice versa, sometimes making up words as he went along. He filled the earth "with cursing cries and deep exclaims" in *Richard III*. In *King Lear* he has Edgar say about Lear that "he childed as I fathered," meaning that Lear's children were like Edgar's father—completely turning around the meaning of "to father." (Because Edgar turns out to be far wiser than his father, this turn of phrase fits perfectly into the play.) And sometimes, as in the statement, "I will description the matter to you, if you be capacity of it," from *The Merry Wives of Windsor*, his characters seemed unable to grasp the differences between parts of speech at all.

So why does William Shakespeare get away with what would have earned us a failing grade in English comp? The answer is a single word— poetry. To work onstage, Shakespeare's lines had to have a certain rhythm. The word choice didn't matter so much as the meter. When you hear those convoluted questions and comments spoken aloud, you begin to understand the genius that was Shakespeare. They sounded right, and to Elizabethan audiences, that's all that really mattered.

~58~

If Mom only knew

Most modern-day parents would be thrilled to find their teenagers reading Shakespeare. After all, the man's a literary icon. Anything William Shakespeare has to say is bound to be more significant and uplifting than rap lyrics. So why worry when the kids pick up a copy of *Romeo and Juliet*? It's great literature, right?

Not so fast, Mom and Dad. Take a closer look at Shakespeare. In addition to his frequent depictions of the older generation as foolish or corrupt, some of his lines are downright vulgar. If a word like *whoreson* doesn't stop you in your tracks, maybe all his allusions to bodily functions and sexual intercourse will. Elizabethans were a lot less hung up on making open references to sex and body parts than we are, and Shakespeare's language shows it. Today we put this playwright's works in a category labeled "highbrow." In his own time, he would have been considered anything but. Shakespeare wrote for public playhouses where the common people went to be entertained. They loved bawdy language, double entendres, and men and women caught in ridiculous situations—the more embarrassing the better. To succeed as a playwright in those days, you had to provide plenty of bathroom humor. And Shakespeare did.

In today's socially correct lexicon, some of Shakespeare's phrasing might actually border on pornographic. That is, if you can understand what he was trying to say. A lot of Shakespeare's sexual innuendoes are presented in ways only an Elizabethan could love. We often miss them because words that we use every day had completely different meanings in Shakespeare's time. Take the word *will*. We think of it as a synonym for self-control or the name of a legal document read after a person's death. In Shakespeare's day it meant sexual desire. And while you might easily figure out that when Shakespeare used words such as *cock*, *organ*, *prick*, and *shaft*, he was referring to male genitalia, his use of *apricot*, *bugle*, *holy-thistle*, *talent*, and *yard* for the same might not be so obvious. Words such as *banquet*, *execution*, *ferret*, *tillage*, and *voyage* sound innocuous to us, but from Shakespeare's pen, they all referred to sexual intercourse or orgasm. Who knew?

The words *die* and *arise* were two of Shakespeare's favorite euphemisms. When, in *Antony and Cleopatra*, Enobarbus utters the line, "Under a compelling occasion, let women die," it's probably safe to assume he wasn't referring solely to female mortality. Elizabethans believed that the release of fluids during intercourse shortened a person's life, so to die in this case probably meant to have a few orgasms first. The word *under*, which likely denotes a sexual position, helps give this one away. Likewise, Elizabethans used the word *arise* to mean one of two things: "stand up" or "have an erection." Knowing Shakespeare's penchant for the double entendre, it's a sure bet that lovestruck Titania wasn't simply rousing donkey-headed Bottom out of a sound sleep in *A Midsummer Night's Dream* when she said, "Arise, arise."

Because slang has changed so much since Shakespeare's time, today's teens poring over reading assignments probably won't appreciate every joke, which may or may not be a good thing. Maybe they'd clamor to read *Hamlet*, *Twelfth Night*, or *Othello* if they knew what the author really meant to say. When it comes to dirty doublespeak, Eminem and *Saturday Night Live* have nothing on William Shakespeare.

~ 59 ~
Didn't I just say that?

Watching a Shakespearean play can feel like déjà vu. You know you've never seen this one before, but you can't shake the feeling of familiarity. The words ring a bell and well they should. Even if you've never read a word of Shakespeare in your life, you've been speaking his language for years.

Madison Avenue would have loved William Shakespeare. He was an advertising copywriter just waiting to happen. Imagine what his knack for the memorable turn of phrase might have done for the sale of soft drinks, pickup trucks, or pharmaceuticals. Without doubt, Shakespeare had an ear for language, which is just one reason why we still quote him almost every day without even knowing it. Some of his turns of phrase have crept into our vernacular, so when you hear one of his characters deliver a line onstage, you can't help but turn to the person next to you and whisper, "Didn't I just say the same thing yesterday?"

Maybe Shakespeare himself had an inkling that his work would live for centuries. After all, he coined the phrase "household words" (*Henry V*). Could he have had a "fatal vision" (*Macbeth*) or "a foregone conclusion" (*Othello*), "for goodness sake" (*Henry VIII*)? In his "heart of hearts" (*Hamlet*) did he find "cold comfort" (*King John*) in an audience's appreciation of his words? Or was public acceptance for Will Shakespeare a matter of "neither here nor there" (*Othello*)?

If you've always shied away from Shakespeare and think you've successfully avoided him until now, think again. The odds are pretty good that the two of you have been cheek-to-cheek for years. Ever told a knock-knock joke? You're quoting *Macbeth*. Called something an "eyesore"? That's from *The Taming of the Shrew*. Fallen prey to the "green-eyed monster"? You're in good company with *Othello*. Approached a situation with "bated breath"? Say hello to *The Merchant of Venice*. "Played fast and loose" or longed for "the naked truth"? Both expressions are from *Love's Labor's Lost*.

Later writers found inspiration in Shakespeare's words, too. Aldous Huxley used "brave new world" from *The Tempest* as the title for his 1932 futuristic novel. And William Faulkner didn't just pull the phrase "sound and fury" right out of thin air. *Macbeth* had uttered those very words centuries before they became part of a 1929 book title.

William Shakespeare is everywhere these days. In fact, so many of the phrases we use on a daily basis have come from his pen it's tempting to credit him with words he never wrote. In *The Merchant of Venice*, Shakespeare told us, "All that glisters is not gold," but he never called "the love of money the root of all evil." Credit for that phrase goes to Saint Paul (1 Timothy 6:10). And while Shakespeare did have something to say about fools, it was not about their tendency to "rush in where angels fear to tread." The poet Alexander Pope gets credit for that one. Shakespeare's comment was, "Lord, what fools these mortals be!" in *A Midsummer Night's Dream*.

PART IV

The Plays

All the world's a stage.
—AS YOU LIKE IT

139

The Play's the Thing

William Shakespeare was an actor and a poet, but it is as a playwright that we remember him best. Over the course of a twenty-five-year writing career, spent mostly in London, he wrote all or part of thirty-nine plays. The histories, comedies, tragedies, and romances he penned are filled with memorable characters, vivid language, timeless plots, and universal themes that made him both a popular playwright in his own time and a literary icon in ours.

How did he do it? What drove William Shakespeare to write in different genres and leave his indelible stamp on each one? Where did he get his ideas; and why, when he brought them to the stage, did he choose to make this one a comedy and that one a tragedy?

Many playwrights, including some who knew William Shakespeare firsthand, have come and gone over the last 400 years. But it is Shakespeare we remember, Shakespeare we revere. We study him in our schools, we quote him more often than any other writer. Why? What is it about this player-turned-playwright that continues to tax our brains and touch our hearts?

CROSSING LINES

Shakespeare's plays can be classified into four categories: history, comedy, tragedy, and romance. Even so, some things about his work either defy classification or cross its individual lines. It's interesting to note that some of the works we might today consider less appealing—such as *Titus Andronicus*—were crowd pleasers in Shakespeare's time. Today, that particular play is almost never performed because it's so violent, yet in Shakespeare's day, theatergoers loved it. Clearly, tastes have changed.

⟨60⟩

Making sense of it all

Blame it on the dynamic duo of John Heminges and Henry Condell. William Shakespeare never tried to pigeonhole his playscripts by genre; his good friends and colleagues John and Henry did it for him. When they put together the first definitive collection of Shakespeare's plays in 1623—the famous *First Folio*—they assigned each to one of three broad categories: comedies, histories, and tragedies, with *Troilus and Cressida* in limbo between the latter two. For years we just assumed *Cymbeline* should be put on a par with *Hamlet*, *The Tempest* lumped in with *As You Like It*, and as for *Troilus and Cressida*, well, we couldn't quite figure out what to think about that. Some classifications didn't seem to make sense, but what did we know about such things?

Scholars now believe that Shakespeare's dramatic works should be apportioned among four divisions instead of three—histories, comedies, tragedies, and romances. Although the lines between them aren't always clear, they at least give us a reasonable frame of reference.

The histories are pretty easy to identify because they are the plays titled solely with the name of an English king. The exceptions to this rule are, of course, *King Lear* and *Macbeth*. Both were kings, one English, one Scottish, but their stories, as told by Shakespeare, are less about history and more about individual character flaws, so they are slotted into the tragedy category instead. Likewise, Shakespeare's plays about Roman rulers, *Julius Caesar*, *Antony and Cleopatra*, and *Coriolanus*, are considered tragedies, not histories.

Shakespeare's histories, of which there are eleven, span a period of England's past beginning with King John in 1200 and closing with Henry VIII in 1547. In between are three other Henrys (IV, V, and VI), two Richards (II and III), and an Edward (III). While each of these rulers has his element of tragedy, Shakespeare focuses on the monarchy as much as the man, preferring to concentrate on a sequence of historical events rather than on a single person.

The histories are relatively simple to categorize, but Shakespeare's comedies, which account for a third of his plays, are somewhat more difficult. For the most part, they have happy endings, but they're not exactly knee slappers, at least not by modern standards. In Shakespeare's world, the comedy centers largely on relationships between men and women; illusions, rivalries, disguises, and cases of mistaken identity are used to drive both the plots and the laughs. Typically, by the end of the play, the lovers are married, although in three of Shakespeare's comedies, tragedy looms large and the promise of marriage is not absolutely assured.

Shakespeare wrote comedies all through his career. The first five— *The Two Gentlemen of Verona*, *The Comedy of Errors*, *The Taming of the Shrew*, *Love's Labor's Lost*, and *A Midsummer's Night's Dream*—were written early, probably between 1593 and 1596. Another five, including *The Merry Wives of Windsor*, which was written at the request of Queen Elizabeth, were penned before 1602. After that date, Shakespeare's comedy took a slightly darker turn; the three comedies written between 1602 and 1608—*All's Well That Ends Well*, *Measure for Measure*, and *Troilus and Cressida*—came to be known as the "problem plays" because they were not quite comedies, but not quite tragedies either.

While histories and comedies comprise more than half of Shakespeare's dramatic output, it is in the tragedy genre that he truly shines. In *Hamlet*, *Othello*, *Macbeth*, and *King Lear*, he gave us tragic heroes with whom we could readily identify. Four tragedies were written during the reign of Elizabeth I, six while James I was on the throne. With *Titus Andronicus*, *Romeo and Juliet*, and *Julius Caesar*, all composed before 1600, Shakespeare practiced his craft; with *Antony and Cleopatra*, *Coriolanus*, *Hamlet*, *Othello*, *King Lear*, and *Macbeth*, he perfected it.

Next to the histories, Shakespeare's tragedies are the easiest to spot. While the histories take us back in time to witness specific events, the tragedies take us into the minds and hearts of the people who lived them. We learn their fears and motivations and we witness their struggles and, ultimately, their tragic downfalls. At the same time, we can always discern a wider context in which these protagonists act. The tragedies are not always easy to watch, but they are, indisputably, the Shakespearean works we remember most.

Four of Shakespeare's last plays—*Pericles*, *Cymbeline*, *The Winter's Tale*, and *The Tempest*—are now often categorized as romances. These storybook adventures, which for years had no separate classification of their own, combine elements of comedy and tragedy to examine broad-based themes centering on jealousy, death, and relations between parents and their children. They end happily, but only after the protagonists and their families undergo a reawakening that is the outgrowth of external action rather than internal reflection.

ᴄ*61*~

Bringing order out of chaos

If Shakespeare had a plan for his writing career, we'll never know it. He seems to have jumped from one genre to the next and then back again with no apparent rhyme or reason and certainly no pattern. We can't even figure out what he wrote when.

Here's what we do know: Between 1587 (we think) and 1613, Shakespeare wrote thirty-nine plays (or thirty-six, depending on which ones you count). He started with the histories (we think), wrote a comedy and a tragedy, then dashed off a couple of narrative poems and a bunch of sonnets before resuming his career as a playwright, producing a slew of comedies, several more histories, and some incredible tragedies. It looks as though he wound the whole thing up by penning a few romances and a couple of collaborative pieces, before retiring in luxury to his hometown of Stratford. As far as firm facts, that's as good as it gets.

Now crack open a book about Shakespeare and what do you see? Somewhere toward the back, you're likely to find a detailed chronology of his works, including the years in which each one was written. If all we know about Shakespeare's writing life is vague generality, how did the authors of these books come up with dates? By pooling three kinds of evidence.

In all likelihood, they looked first for documentary evidence: written records of performance or publication dates, perhaps even a quarto version of a particular play. But even though documentation such as this is helpful, it may have little bearing on the date the play was actually written. Plays were sometimes performed for the first time years after they were written, and given that companies rarely released a play to a printer until it was deemed no longer commercially viable, publication dates weren't much help either. A quarto edition of *Love's Labor's Lost*, for example, was printed in 1598, but scholars believe the play may have been written as many as five years before that.

Dialogue within the play itself can sometimes be used to pinpoint a date, if it refers to a real person or event, but even that can be misleading. Shakespeare was known to "telescope" history—clump events together for dramatic effect even though they occurred in real time several years apart. A passage in *The Comedy of Errors*, for example, refers to the French civil war, which ended in 1593. That's not much help for dating a play, considering the war lasted from 1589 to 1593 and the reference might have been added long after the war was over.

Some scholars believe they can determine the logical progression of Shakespeare's work based on a study of his style. Common sense says a writer's style should mature over time, but for someone as clever as Shakespeare, assumptions about maturity can be a tough call. His earliest comedies have certain stylistic elements in common—elaborate rhyme schemes and lots of puns, for example—that would suggest a beginning writer. But in *Love's Labor's Lost*, believed to be fourth in a string of his comedies beginning with *The Two Gentlemen of Verona*, Shakespeare uses poetic excess to make a point, which suggests a writer who was sure of himself and his craft.

So when it comes to knowing which came first—*The Comedy of Errors* or *The Taming of the Shrew*—our best guess is exactly that: a guess. Shakespeare took the truth with him to his grave.

⹎62⹏

Where does he come up with this stuff?

Necessity may be the mother of invention, but William Shakespeare found a better way. When he needed a plot or a character, he didn't invent anything; he pulled it from another source. That's not to say he wasn't creative or he didn't have a boatload of talent to draw on. He just knew where to best expend his energy. If Plutarch had already invented a decent plot, why should he spend time inventing another one? He had audiences hungry for new dramas and no time to waste.

Shakespeare derived plots from a variety of sources, including folklore, mythology, histories, classical drama, and even popular romances. And although he *could* have lifted them, word for word—there were no laws against plagiarism in those days and everybody did it—Shakespeare chose not to. And with good reason. He had a keen eye for the tale that could best be transferred from page to stage. When he found one he liked, he took the basic story behind the words someone else had written, then turned it, twisted it, set it upside down, and made it his own. Sometimes, especially when the story was true, as in the case of King Lear, he used a combination of historical sources to craft his plot and mold his characters. He had his favorites, of course: Plutarch's *Lives of the Noble Greeks and Latins* for his Roman plays, *Julius Caesar, Antony and Cleopatra,* and *Coriolanus*; Raphael Holinshed's *The Chronicles of*

England, Ireland and Scotland for his English histories. For his comedies, tragedies, and romances, he was more likely to conceive his work from a single, favorite piece of fiction. Like a creative cook who starts with a basic recipe, he added extra seasonings and extracts that would transform an otherwise ordinary dish into something special.

In the case of *Othello*, Shakespeare began with Cinthio's *Hecatommithi*. He added a teaspoon of motive, a dash of psychological intrigue, and a pinch of villainy, then tossed it all together and served it up on a bed of beautiful poetry. The result was pure creative genius, even groundbreaking social commentary. Even his comedies, which should have been strictly for fun, had unusual depth. The plot for *As You Like It* was lifted from the popular 1590 romance *Rosalynde* by Thomas Lodge. In Shakespeare's hands, the original, which is a pretty straightforward tale, became a multilayered comic love story of incredible depth.

As much as Shakespeare's plots delight us, it is his characters we remember most. He created more than 1,200 of them and nearly everyone who's ever read Shakespeare can remember at least one or two. And although his characters speak a brand of English we sometimes find difficult to comprehend, we can immediately identify with their actions and motivations. They are like us: human beings who love and laugh and sometimes get caught up in improbable situations or are forced to make impossible choices. We know these people and we have felt their pain. We almost certainly will never kill a king, but we understand why Macbeth does. And while we may not condone the act or agree with his reasons, we embrace his guilt and recoil with the same kind of horror when the deed is done. We've walked in Hamlet's shoes; we know what it's like to suspect the worst. Because we remember the sting of first love gone wrong, we can relate to Romeo and Juliet.

As far as we know, William Shakespeare never had any formal training in creative writing. What he did have was an instinctive understanding of basic human nature and how best to portray it. Which is why, 400 years after his death, we can read his plays and still find something in them that we can relate to and appreciate.

~*63*~
Lost in translation

How do we know for certain that when we read one of Shakespeare's plays today, we're reading the words he actually wrote? The short answer is that we don't. Surprisingly, the confusion began while Shakespeare was still alive. Thanks to shady publishing practices and the nature of play production in Elizabethan times, the printed scripts of Shakespeare's works sometimes strayed a long way from the original within just a few years of their creation.

We have no way of knowing, of course, exactly how Shakespeare worked—how many drafts he produced, for example—but we can presume that, at some point in the writing process, he would have deemed a play good enough to turn over to his acting company. The minute he did that, he pretty much lost all control of the work. This first copy, called "foul papers," would have contained the full script, but usually no detailed stage directions. If legible enough, it would have been passed directly on to the Master of Revels, who would have reviewed it for sensitive political or religious references. If not, a playhouse scribe would have recopied the script to create a second, more legible version known as "fair papers." In either case, once the papers passed muster with the Master of Revels, the next step would have been for the acting company to create another copy called the prompt-book. Since this version of the script was used by the players for rehearsals, it would have contained detailed notes about stage directions, sound effects, and the like.

In Shakespeare's time, playwrights wrote for performance, not for publication. Although an acting company could have turned over any one of these versions—foul papers, fair papers, or prompt-book—to a printer, it was not in the company's best interest to do so, unless (1) the play was no longer popular, and its publication was the only way for the company to still make some money from it; (2) a pirated version of the play had already been published, and a more accurate version could earn the company additional cash; or (3) the company was about to go belly-up and had to sell its inventory of plays to stay afloat. From time to time, a playwright might step out on a limb and sell his work directly to a printer, regardless of his arrangement with an acting company. There is no evidence, however, that Shakespeare ever did this; in fact, as far as his plays are concerned, he seems to have remained pretty oblivious to the whole publishing process throughout much of his life.

Plays published as individual works in Elizabethan times were referred to as quartos, so named because the printers' sheets were folded twice to produce a book that was approximately the size of our trade paperbacks. Plays printed from authorized scripts—usually foul papers or prompt-books—were called "good quartos." "Bad quartos" were those printed from scripts that had been stolen from theater companies or, more often, simply reconstructed by actors from memory and set down on paper by a scribe who worked for the printer. (Did you actually think pirating of performances originated with the VCR?) Since there were no copyright laws in those days, printing an unauthorized version of a play was perfectly legal. The only recourse the play's owners would have had was to follow up the pirated version with a more accurate copy of their own.

Approximately eighteen of Shakespeare's plays were published as quartos during his lifetime; some were good, some bad. Interestingly, none were divided into acts or scenes, because on the Elizabethan stage, divisions were not considered necessary; a new scene was simply indicated by a blank stage, which would have been obvious to an audience.

Printed versions of Shakespeare's plays that appear to have been created from memory include bad quartos of *Romeo and Juliet, Henry*

V, and *The Merry Wives of Windsor*. Subsequent quartos of these works contained title pages bearing the inscription "newly corrected and augmented," indicating the acting company may have made an attempt to recoup a portion of its investment by releasing authorized versions.

Typically, plays reproduced from memory were not terribly accurate. The story line might be correct, but individual lines were sometimes misplaced or even attributed to the wrong character. An example of a bad quarto created from memory was the 1603 publication of *Hamlet*, in which appears the familiar soliloquy with a not-so-familiar opening line: "To be, or not to be, I there's the point." Subsequent quartos, printed from either the foul papers or prompt-book, contain the words we recognize: "To be, or not to be, that is the question."

~ 64 ~

Lost in time and space

It was an accident waiting to happen. What with foul papers, fair papers, prompt-books, and good and bad quartos for Shakespeare's plays all floating around London at the same time, sooner or later something was bound to get lost. Sadly, at least one, and possibly as many as three, of the plays we think Shakespeare wrote have disappeared altogether.

The one Shakespearean work we're pretty sure is missing is a play titled *Cardenio*. Little is known about this play except that it might take its plot from an episode in the great Spanish epic *Don Quixote* by Miguel de Cervantes. Although we can't know for certain when the play was written, we do have a pretty good idea about when it was last performed. Surviving documentation indicates that on May 20, 1613, John Heminges, who was in charge of the King's Men at that time, received a sum of money for the performance of six plays. *Cardenio* was one of the six. By this time, John Fletcher had succeeded Shakespeare as chief playwright for the King's Men and the two had already collaborated twice to create *Henry VIII* and *The Two Noble Kinsmen*. Fletcher is known to have been an admirer of Cervantes, so it's possible he and Shakespeare may have written *Cardenio* together.

After the 1613 reference to the play, all mention of it disappears until 1728, when Lewis Theobald published a play titled *Double Falsehood, or The Distressed Lovers*. The title page of that play notes that it is based on the story of *Cardenio*, "revised and adapted" from the play "originally written by William Shakespeare." End of story. There are no further mentions, and *Cardenio* is still missing in action.

A second play attributed at least in part to Shakespeare, *Sir Thomas More*, is also missing . . . well, sort of. A few pages of the script survive, including 147 lines thought to be in Shakespeare's own handwriting. Some believe this is an indication that Shakespeare wrote the play; others do not accept the snippet of penmanship as conclusive proof. Shortly after the play was written in 1595, it was banned, and some believe that Shakespeare, who by then was well regarded as a playwright in London theater circles, may have been brought in to rewrite the offending controversial scene. That would explain why only a small portion of the surviving script is in Shakespeare's hand. In any event, *Sir Thomas More* has never been officially incorporated into the Shakespearean canon.

The third candidate thought to belong to the realm of the missing is a play that may have never existed at all. A 1598 treatise by Francis Meres credits Shakespeare with a play titled *Love's Labour's Won*, which some scholars believe was a sequel to *Love's Labor's Lost*, and which no one else seems to have ever seen. If there is such a play, scholars believe it's not missing at all. Shakespeare simply gave it a new title before it went into production, and we know it today as *The Taming of the Shrew*, *Much Ado About Nothing*, or possibly even *All's Well That Ends Well*.

~ *65* ~

It could be Shakespeare, but then again . . .

If you start looking into the life and work of William Shakespeare, sooner or later you're going to discover that the facts don't always add up. For example, scholars can't seem to agree on the number of plays Shakespeare actually wrote. Some say thirty-nine; others say only thirty-six. What's more frustrating, especially if you're trying to figure out the order in which Shakespeare wrote his plays, is that even the people who have devoted their lives to studying such things have reached different conclusions about which plays are in dispute.

At particular issue are these four works: *Edward III*, *Sir Thomas More*, *The Two Noble Kinsmen*, and *Pericles*. Depending on which source you consult, you may see one or two of these works listed in a chronology of Shakespeare's plays, or you may see none at all.

The trouble with deciding which plays Shakespeare wrote and when dates clear back to 1623, when John Heminges and Henry Condell put together the first "definitive" collection of the author's works under one cover. They narrowed their selection down to fourteen comedies, ten histories, and eleven tragedies, plus *Troilus and Cressida*, which didn't seem to quite fit into any genre.

Things were going along swimmingly until they got to *Pericles*. Heminges and Condell had already discounted *Edward III* and *The Two Noble Kinsmen*. The latter was a collaboration with John Fletcher, and even though Shakespeare might have worked on *Edward III*, an awful lot of the words didn't sound like his. That left only *Pericles*. It seemed quite different from Shakespeare's other works, but then again, so did *The Winter's Tale* and *The Tempest*, written during the latter period of his life. The real sticking point with *Pericles*, however, was that they couldn't seem to lay their hands on the most accurate text. Shakespeare wasn't around anymore to advise them, so rather than risk printing an unauthorized version, they nixed the play completely. The *First Folio* went to press without *Pericles*. It would be another forty years before the play was finally published in the *Third Folio* and thus officially incorporated into the Shakespeare canon.

The other three plays in question never appeared in any of the four *Folios*. *The Two Noble Kinsman*, although written in collaboration with John Fletcher, was later accepted as a Shakespeare work. After all, Fletcher and Shakespeare had also collaborated on *Henry VIII* (Heminges and Condell possibly didn't know that, or they might have omitted it from their *First Folio* just on basic principle).

Edward III was only recently added to the official Shakespeare canon—by some scholars. Long thought to be the work of some anonymous actors or stagehands to which Shakespeare might have contributed only a small portion, it may have been written out of jealousy toward a rival playwright. *Edward III* was first published in 1596, but because of the way Scots were treated in the play, it was banned when, following the death of Queen Elizabeth, James VI of Scotland ascended to the English throne as James I of England.

Meanwhile, *Sir Thomas More* still remains largely outside the accepted Shakespeare canon. It was banned almost as soon as it was written and there is some question as to whether it was ever actually staged at all. As mentioned in the previous point, the surviving pages include several lines believed to be in Shakespeare's hand. If so, they would represent the only example we have of his handwriting outside of legal documents.

One additional interesting bit of trivia: The *Third Folio* (1663) credits Shakespeare with writing seven plays attributed to anonymous playwrights, including *Locrine* (1594), *The London Prodigal* (1605), and *A Yorkshire Tragedy*. All were later determined not to be Shakespeare's; they were removed from the *Third Folio* when it was reprinted in 1664.

～66～

Together at last

Unlike his contemporary Ben Jonson, who released his own collection of favorite works in 1616, Shakespeare made no attempt to publish the plays he wrote. Fortunately, he had friends who took it upon themselves to do so. In 1623, seven years after the author's death, John Heminges and Henry Condell, two of Shakespeare's colleagues from the King's Men, edited and assembled the first complete collection of his plays. Titled *First Folio* because of its size (the printers' sheets were folded only once), it contained thirty-six of the thirty-nine plays eventually credited to Shakespeare, eighteen of which were being published for the first time. As explained in Number 65, *Edward III*, *Pericles*, *The Two Noble Kinsmen*, and *Sir Thomas More* are all noticeably missing. Of these, only *Pericles* would show up in a subsequent collection, the *Third Folio*, published in 1663.

For the *First Folio*, Heminges and Condell divided the plays into three broad sections: comedies (fourteen), histories (ten), and tragedies (eleven); *Troilus and Cressida*, which appears to have been added late in the production process, was separately paged and placed between the histories and tragedies. Within the three sections, only the histories seem to be in any logical order; *King John*, who ruled the earliest among Shakespeare's monarchs, gets first billing.

In addition to the plays, the *First Folio* contains three more notable elements. The title page features what has become the most recognizable image of Shakespeare—the Droeshout portrait. Another interesting component is a list of the members of Shakespeare's acting company who presumably would have played the roles in the original productions of these thirty-six plays. The list includes Shakespeare himself, as well as Richard Burbage and the famed comic actors Will Kempe and Robert Armin.

What is most significant about the *First Folio*, however, is that it provides the most conclusive evidence we have of which plays William Shakespeare most certainly wrote. Heminges and Condell, as members of Shakespeare's acting company when it was still known as the Lord Chamberlain's Men, would have known Shakespeare for most of his life as a playwright, and they would have had firsthand knowledge about which plays he actually wrote. For the sake of protecting their friend's reputation, they would have certainly also made reasonable attempts to include the most precise version of each work. Good quartos would have been compared against foul papers or prompt-books to ensure accuracy; bad quartos would have been disregarded altogether.

By the way, the purchase price for *First Folio* when it was first released in 1623 was £1 (the equivalent of about $50 today). Only 1,000 copies were printed, of which approximately 200 survive, fourteen of which are said to be in near-perfect condition. Should you happen to come across one, be prepared to shell out big bucks. A *First Folio* in mint condition today goes for more than $1 million.

～ 67 ～

You mean I *wrote that?*

John Heminges and Henry Condell may have thought they were doing the world a favor when they published the first authorized collection of Shakespeare's plays in 1623, but what they really did was open the proverbial can of worms. In the 380-odd years since the release of the *First Folio*, editors have had a field day with those scripts—adding a line here, deleting a word there, changing punctuation, capitalization, and spelling to such a degree that it's entirely possible Shakespeare himself wouldn't recognize portions of his own work.

If ever an argument was needed for stringent copyright laws, what has happened to Shakespeare's work over 400 years provides one. Between good quartos, bad quartos, and four *Folios*, there are so many versions of *Hamlet* floating around it's practically impossible to know which one really came from Shakespeare's hand. You'd think you could trust the good quarto and the *First Folio*, but even those so-called reliable sources didn't always agree. In one, a fat weed "roots" itself; in the other the weed "rots" itself. Either could be correct, but which one is it really?

And let's not even get started on *King Lear*. Differences between the *First Folio* and 1608 quarto texts alone are enough to drive an editor over the edge. The *Folio* text contains 100 lines not in the quarto; not to be outdone, the quarto contains 300 lines not in the Folio. For years, editors accepted the *First Folio* text as definitive, but then someone suggested the two versions might actually be independent plays. This prompted a flurry of articles, conferences, and letters to the editors of various scholarly journals. The argument still hasn't been resolved.

Even plays like *Macbeth*, for which there is only one widely accepted version, manage to engender controversy. When the lines "I dare do all that may become a man, / Who dares no more, is none?" first appeared in print, editors working on a later text for publication assumed "no" was a typo and changed it to "do." Were they right? Maybe this same flick of an editor's pencil is what made Hamlet wish for his "too, too sullied flesh to melt" in one collection of Shakespeare's works and his "too, too solid flesh" in another. Or turned music from the "food" to the "fool" of love in various versions of *As You Like It*.

When it comes to setting down the words Shakespeare wrote, editors wield a lot of power. If there's more than one text available for a play, it's up to the editor to select the most definitive version, then compare it to the others and make adjustments. Getting inside this creative genius's head is a daunting task. Did Shakespeare mean to put a question mark after that "no"? Or should it be an exclamation point? Should that single word go on a line by itself or be wrapped into the rest of the dialogue? Deciding either way could change not just the way the words sound when they are spoken, but the entire meaning of a passage.

Lest you think editors are messing with Shakespeare purely for the sake of messing, consider this. The whole let's-tamper-with-Shakespeare movement got started with a couple of typesetters even before the *First Folio* ever went to press; later editors identified the problem and corrected it. Typesetter A, it seems, was careful and methodical. Typesetter B, on the other hand, apparently liked to carry strings of words around in his head for a while before setting them in type and, well, you can imagine what happened. Words—sometimes even whole lines—were misplaced or forgotten. Thanks to the eagle eyes of editors over the years, the missing pieces have been restored and Shakespeare lives on in a reasonably authentic version . . . we hope.

~68~

The Italy conundrum

As far as we know, William Shakespeare never went to Italy. Yet five of the plays he is supposed to have written between 1592 and 1594 are set there. The details about Venice, Verona, Messina (in Sicily), and Padua that he included in the scripts for *The Two Gentlemen of Verona*, *The Taming of the Shrew*, *The Merchant of Venice*, *Much Ado About Nothing*, and *Romeo and Juliet* are so vivid; surely Shakespeare must have seen those places first-hand. Or did he? This question has puzzled Shakespearean scholars.

Some believe the playwright never crossed the channel. By 1592, Shakespeare was just beginning to make a name for himself as a playwright, which means, from a financial point of view, he was barely getting by. In Elizabethan times, only the very wealthy could afford to travel abroad for pleasure. Besides, Italy was the seat of Catholicism, and given that Queen Elizabeth was such a staunch Protestant, it would not have been the smartest choice for a vacation destination, at least not if you hoped to secure her favor. The pope was considered a particularly powerful figure in those days, and to venture into his territory would be to take a chance on becoming "infected" by Papism. No up-and-coming young Englishman of property or means would have wanted to risk the official scrutiny that a holiday in Italy might have drawn.

On the other hand, 1592 is the year London theaters were shut down because of the plague and Shakespeare took a patron, the Earl of Southampton. Some scholars think that the earl may have visited northern Italy and that he took Shakespeare with him. Southampton certainly had the money and clout to travel, and it wouldn't have been unusual for him to take his protégé along. Certainly, the timing was about right. Surviving records from the period show that Shakespeare was under Southampton's patronage from 1592 to 1594.

Nevertheless, the other side counters with evidence to indicate that Shakespeare wouldn't have needed to see Italy firsthand to gather knowledge of the country. He might simply have spent time talking to Southampton's secretary and language tutor, John Florio. A former professor of languages at Oxford University and the son of an Italian Protestant refugee who had settled in London, Florio was then working on the Italian-English dictionary he would publish in 1598. Perhaps over tea and crumpets, Shakespeare pumped Florio for the details about Venice and the Veneto that he would later incorporate into his plays. It's also possible that Shakespeare could have gleaned his information about Italy by conversing with travelers recently returned from sojourns there or with Italian citizens who were visiting London. The Oliphant, an inn in London's Bankside neighborhood, was known to have attracted an Italian clientele; Shakespeare might have stopped in there on his way to and from the theater. Or maybe he got his information from Emilia Bassano, the young woman of Venetian descent who was rumored to be Shakespeare's Dark Lady (see Number 91).

The Oxfordians (see Number 23) claim the Italian expertise demonstrated in the plays is further proof that Shakespeare's work is actually Edward de Vere's, since de Vere is known to have traveled to Italy.

Whether he went to Italy or not, Shakespeare's grasp of the finer details concerning its topography seems to be a little shaky. In *The Two Gentlemen of Verona*, his characters depart the town by ship, whereas the real Verona is landlocked. So is Padua, but in *The Taming of the Shrew*, Biondello somehow comes ashore. While Shakespeare may not have had all his details correct, he did accomplish one important thing for Italy: He put Verona on the map. To this day, visitors flock there to see a balcony purported to have figured prominently in *Romeo and Juliet* (there's no proof, by the way, that it did).

~ *69* ~
Witches and fairies and ghosts . . . oh my!

Shakespeare filled his plays with supernatural creatures. There were fairies such as Oberon and Titania in *A Midsummer Night's Dream*, spirits such as Ariel in *The Tempest*, and witches such as the three weird sisters in *Macbeth*. And who can forget that scary ghost of Hamlet's father?

Despite the efforts of organized Christianity to wipe out all remnants of paganism and the occult, traditions held over from Celtic folklore remained strong in Shakespeare's time. Many Elizabethans believed in witches, apparitions, and tiny creatures who came out at night solely for the purpose of playing nasty tricks on people. Shakespeare leveraged these beliefs to great advantage in his works—sometimes to lighten the mood and other times so he could drive home a serious point.

The sprites who attend the fairy queen, Titania, in *A Midsummer Night's Dream* are most definitely bent on mischief, but not the malevolent kind. With names like Peaseblossom, Cobweb, Moth, and Mustardseed, how could they be mean? Boys with singing and dancing skills would have played these parts in Shakespeare's day, and the audience would have loved their antics. The weird sisters of *Macbeth*, on the other hand, would have received quite a different reception. In Shakespeare's time, witches were greatly feared, and these three, with their strange chants and simmering soup full of gruesome ingredients, would have seemed both the epitome of evil and all too horribly real.

So would the ghost of Hamlet's father. In this day of ghoulish movie soundtracks and computerized special effects, it's hard to imagine that the sight of an apparition, supposedly returning from purgatory but actually rising from a trapdoor in the floor of the stage, could strike terror in an audience; but in Elizabethan times, it probably did. At the very least, it would have shut them up, which may be exactly what the author intended. The deafening silence that accompanied the ghost's appearance would have given the actor, whom many believe may have been

Shakespeare himself, the chance to be heard. Elizabethan audiences were known to be rowdy. The return of beings from the beyond might have been little more than an effective ploy Shakespeare used to get the crowd to settle down and listen, although in this case it's also a great device for building suspense, because the Elizabethan audience wouldn't have known if the ghost was telling the truth about his own death.

THE HISTORIES

Tied to time and place, Shakespeare's eleven history plays re-create the people and events of England's turbulent past in a way that no teachers and textbooks ever could.

70

Putting the past in perspective

William Shakespeare started and ended his writing career with plays about history. Over the course of twenty-five years, he wrote eleven of them, though not in chronological order. It's possible to trace nearly 350 years of English history through Shakespeare's plays, but the author himself didn't start at the beginning. The monarch who should have been first, King John, came fifth in Shakespeare's line of literary succession. In his list of writing priorities, the author put Henry VI before Henrys IV and V and Richard III before II. We're not sure why, but it doesn't really matter. Although events and some names overlap between plays, you can read or watch them as individual works or as pieces of a sweeping, multi-generational British royal saga.

Why Shakespeare focused his early dramatic efforts on history is a mystery. Maybe he was sick and tired of seeing Greek and Roman history acted out onstage. Maybe, caught up in the patriotic fervor of his day, he decided it was England's turn to shine. After all, with the forward-thinking Elizabeth I on the throne and Sir Francis Drake on the seas, England was poised to assume a pre-eminent place in a rapidly changing world. It's probably pretty safe to assume that, in his own time, Shakespeare's history plays were the proverbial idea whose time had come. By 1592, England was feeling her oats. The Spanish Armada had been defeated and people were swelling with national pride. Plays extolling the grandeur of a glorious past would have likely been real crowd pleasers.

Or maybe, in the course of his reading, Shakespeare simply came across stories from English history that he thought would make smooth transitions from page to stage. Whatever the reason, we can be grateful, because Shakespeare's histories, with their timeless themes and unforgettable characters, are among some of his finest works.

Shakespeare's histories are easy to spot; they all carry the name of a king as their title. For purposes of organization, the histories are typically divided into two tetralogies according to the dates in which they are believed to have been written. The first tetralogy includes *Henry VI, Parts I, II,* and *III,* and *Richard III.* These first four were probably written sometime between 1587 and 1592. We don't know an exact date because we don't know for sure what Shakespeare was up to during those years. We assume he arrived in London around 1587; we know for certain he was in the city in 1592 and that he had those plays in hand. The second tetralogy includes *Richard II, Henry IV, Parts I* and *II,* and *Henry V.* These plays were likely written between 1595 and 1599. Now here's where things start to get confusing. The first tetralogy deals with English monarchs who reigned from 1422 to 1485; the second tetralogy is about the kings who ruled before them, from 1377 to 1422. For the sake of continuity and a better appreciation of the historical events around which these plays are built, it's best to read them in chronological order.

Shakespeare's other three plays on English history—*King John, Edward III,* and *Henry VIII*—stand alone. Since they are not part of a series with cross-references among them, you can read each as a self-contained work. Or, if you're a stickler for historical chronology, slip these monarchs in among the others, according to their royal reigns. *King John* and *Edward III* would thus move to the head of the pack and *Henry VIII* would bring up the rear.

Don't shy away from Shakespeare's histories because you're afraid to venture into the murky world of English royal succession. These plays are not so much about names and dates as they are about families in crisis, political schemers, and wartime heroics—subjects to which we all can relate. Shakespeare practically invented this genre, and you'll find that the time you take to appreciate it is time well spent.

～*71*～

But Lear was a king, too

It's difficult to separate Shakespeare's plays into the four distinct categories of history, comedy, tragedy, and romance, and scholars sometimes disagree about where a particular play should be placed because a single work may contain elements of more than one category. The line between history and tragedy can sometimes be especially blurred.

If Shakespeare's histories are defined as plays having to do with real events and real people, then why didn't *Julius Caesar*, *Antony and Cleopatra*, and *Coriolanus* make the cut? They're real people. Well, yes, but they're Romans. Shakespeare's "histories" are about English monarchs.

Well, that makes sense. But what about King Lear? He was a real person, and an English monarch to boot. Why isn't Shakespeare's story about him classified as a history? And while we're on the subject, what about that Scottish king Macbeth?

The answer can be summed up in a single word: treatment. King Lear

and Macbeth, and, oh yes, those Romans, too, have been deemed tragedies because of the way Shakespeare handled their stories. The difference,
in a nutshell, is that histories generally look outward whereas tragedies
usually look inward. Shakespeare's histories focus on the story of a man
caught up in a sequence of extraordinary historical events. And although
these plays are named for English monarchs, it is the events themselves
rather than the royal personage who directed or survived them that take
center stage. Richard III certainly has the makings of a tragic protagonist, but Shakespeare chooses to tell the story of his scheming villainy in
the larger context of British history. In contrast, each of Shakespeare's
tragedies is a tale of one man's struggle against a very personal demon—
ambition, revenge, jealousy, pride. If events of a cosmic nature are taking
place outside of that struggle, we don't know it. Nor should we. Shakespeare wants us to zero in on what happens to the man and not to the
country he rules. It's a fine line to be sure; in some tragedies, the larger
society is as interesting as the protagonist's struggles, and many characters in the histories are as interesting as tragic heroes.

But to get back to the original question—what about King Lear?
We know that Shakespeare pulled the true story of King Lear from two
sources: a contemporary play titled *The True Chronicle History of King Leir*
and Holinshed's *The Chronicles of England, Ireland and Scotland*, which
includes the legend of Lear as part of England's mythic beginnings. But
he must have recognized that while Lear's story was interesting, what
happened to the king didn't change the course of English history. This

was essentially a tale of one man's inability to admit the mistakes he'd made and his descent into madness as a result. William Shakespeare recognized that it would be better told as tragedy than as historical fact, and so we now have one of his most powerful plays.

~72~
What's up with all those Henrys?

More English kings have carried the name Henry than almost any other, and Shakespeare deals with four of them. Seven of his eleven history plays are about Henrys—IV, V, VI, and VIII. Although so many monarchs with the same first name in swift succession seems confusing to us, Elizabethans would have understood it with no trouble. Just as we recognize the names of our presidents (well, maybe not Franklin Pierce or Chester Alan Arthur), Shakespeare's audiences would have had a passing knowledge of their Henrys. And their Richards, too.

For those of us across the pond who grew up with elected heads of state instead of naturally assumed ones, the succession of English crowns can be a tough nut to crack. Not only does everyone seem to have the same first name, some of the characters are called by more than one. In Shakespeare's play *King Henry IV*, the king is alternately referred to as

Bolingbroke, Lancaster, Hereford, and just plain Henry. Keeping it all straight while trying to enjoy a complicated story line is enough to sour even the hardiest playgoers.

It's not necessary to be an expert on British royals before you see one of Shakespeare's history plays, but a little pretheater preparation never hurts. All those Henrys, Edwards, Richards, Johns, Annes, and Margarets become a tad more distinctive when you know something about their backgrounds and where they fit into the larger scheme of things. Crack open a history book and check out the genealogical chart for the English royal houses that ruled between 1377 and 1422, the time period with which the bulk of Shakespeare's histories are concerned. The plots of these plays revolve around intricate family relationships, and it helps to know who is related to who and how. If you don't want to delve too deeply into English history, look up the names Lancaster, Tudor, and York in your nearest user-friendly encyclopedia. Those are the royal houses that struggled to gain and keep the British crown as depicted in Shakespeare's plays. A quick detour to the entry labeled "War of the Roses" will help you understand how it all turned out.

Before you see a performance of one of Shakespeare's histories, read the actual play, too, just to get a feel for the language and a grasp on the names of the people you'll be seeing onstage. Whatever you do, don't try to follow the action by bringing a printed copy of the play to a performance. You'll soon be hopelessly lost. The histories are among Shakespeare's longest plays, so for the sake of today's audiences, with shorter attention spans, directors frequently cut lines and scenes. Just sit back instead and let the words flow out and over you. Before long, English history à la Shakespeare is bound to become clear.

~ *73* ~
Politics couched as history

William Shakespeare was an astute man. He knew the movers and shakers of his day, and he probably had strong opinions about a lot of topics. But he never let them slide into his work, at least not overtly. Scholars have for years debated the idea that, in writing his history plays, Shakespeare may have found a way to express his opinions about current events without seeming to do so. If he was determined to comment about the topics of the day, that would have been a smart way to do it.

History was "fact," and as long as he didn't stray too far from it, he could touch on such topics as the merits of a powerful monarch versus a weak one, the tragedy of civil war, and the motives that drive men to commit acts of good or evil. So according to Shakespeare's interpretation, Richard III, for his faults, comes across as a brave warrior and Richard II, who lost his crown through fault of his own, speaks hauntingly beautiful poetry.

Although Shakespeare appears on the surface to be politically conservative—some have even called him an apologist for the Tudor and Stuart dynasties—there's no concrete proof of where his sympathies lay, except maybe in his treatment of Richard III. After years of double-dealing and a series of bloody atrocities, Richard finally gets his due. He is killed by Richmond, who is subsequently crowned Henry VII. Richard is the monster; Henry VII, Queen Elizabeth's grandfather, is the hero. Hardly surprising when you consider the source of a playwright's bread and butter in those times. If Shakespeare wanted to keep working, he needed to spout the "party line." In order for his plays to be performed, this script and all others had to make it through the censors, who were representatives of the Queen. If, during Elizabeth's reign, Shakespeare's plays portrayed the House of Tudor in the best possible light, he can hardly be blamed. It would have been professional suicide, not to mention downright dangerous, to do otherwise.

~74~
Don't believe everything you read

Shakespeare changed history, or at least what we think we know about it. Was Richard III really a sadistic humpbacked villain who would stop at nothing to secure the throne? Or do we only think so because that's how we've seen him portrayed by Shakespeare?

William Shakespeare has probably done more to shape our visions of English history than any textbook or teacher ever did. His histories bring to life onstage eight British monarchs and nearly 350 of his country's most turbulent years. The events and people he portrayed onstage were real, but his treatment of them was almost always colored by his own interpretations and by the limits of the Elizabethan stage. Shakespeare was a playwright, not a historian, and that is a fact we would do well to remember whenever we see or read one of these plays.

It's not that Shakespeare deliberately handed us the wrong historical facts. Sometimes he just telescoped them, taking events that occurred several years apart and condensing them into a shorter period of time for dramatic effect. In *Henry VI, Part I*, for example, he has Talbot dying at the hands of French forces led by Joan of Arc. In reality, Talbot died in 1453; Joan had been executed twenty-two years before. But no matter. The audience didn't seem to mind, and onstage the whole thing worked.

Shakespeare never meant to teach us history with his plays. He meant to humanize it. He made kings and queens seem real—fathers and mothers who worried about their children; men and women who ate, drank, made love, and then slept; people with public ambitions and private dreams, who were not very different from us. We see the always-commanding Henry IV, who like any father wants his son to settle down, and we are moved by Henry VI as he struggles with the weight of his royal responsibilities and wishes that he could be a simple shepherd.

The stories Shakespeare brought to life onstage would have been familiar to his audience. They would have grown up hearing these tales of murder and mayhem, battle and betrayal, centering on the English royal court. They would have been fascinated to see it all unfold before their very eyes. And they wouldn't have particularly cared if names, dates, and places weren't always quite correct.

Shakespeare's take on history is sometimes as interesting for what it does not include as for what it does. Even though he devotes a play to King John, the monarch who was forced by his barons to sign the Magna Carta, Shakespeare makes no mention of that pivotal event. Nor does he touch on the Black Death, which wiped out a third of England's population during the reign of Edward III. His portrayal of Henry VIII includes only two wives and barely a reference to the English Protestant Reformation this monarch launched.

What does this say about Shakespeare's grasp of history? If there is a lesson to be learned from his plays it is this: Be careful never to confuse real life with the life you see onstage. While history makes for good fiction, fiction doesn't necessarily teach us the truth about our past.

~75~
A friend indeed—but not in deed

Every young prince aspiring to be king should have a friend like Falstaff. More than a mere comic character, Sir John Falstaff is at once a marvel, a spectacle, the perfect foil for a would-be king, and, as second only to Hamlet among Shakespeare's most memorable creations, a veritable sensation. He is the only Shakespearean character to appear in four plays, including one written especially for him.

Falstaff makes his first appearance in *Henry IV, Part I*, where he is cast as Prince Hal's closest friend and confidant. A former knight now gone to seed, he serves as a substitute father figure for the Prince, living by his wits and managing to survive without lifting so much as a finger. He pops up again in *Henry IV, Part II*, still a mentor and close friend of Hal's, although the prince does his best now to distance himself. By the end of the play, when Hal becomes King Henry V, Falstaff has been relegated to the kingly B list. He and his friends are prevented from coming within ten miles of the King, and Falstaff is ultimately arrested and jailed for his crimes. It is perhaps the cruelest moment in this play, but for dramatic effect it is the perfect way for Shakespeare to show Hal's transformation from partying prince to serious monarch. By *Henry V*, Falstaff is an afterthought, his death a mere mention in passing.

Falstaff is one of the most popular characters ever to flow from the tip of Shakespeare's pen. Queen Elizabeth is said to have loved him so much she asked Shakespeare to write a play in which the rotund old scoundrel falls in love. Shakespeare quickly obliged (some reports say the Queen gave him just two weeks) with *The Merry Wives of Windsor*. In this overtly farcical romp, Falstaff is cast as an ambitious rogue mired in debt, who sets out to raise funds by finding himself a rich mistress.

In all cases, Falstaff is cast as both a wit and an amateur philosopher. His appetites for food, drink, and women are legendary, yet he remains a man of intelligence and even a sort of honor. His soliloquy on honor in the midst of the final battle in *Henry IV, Part I* may not be the message that Shakespeare wanted his audience to go home with, but it's one of the most memorable speeches of the play. A brief sample: "What is honor? A word. What is in the word 'honor'? . . . Air. A trim reckoning! Who hath it? He that died o' Wednesday. Doth he feel it? No."

Shakespeare intended originally for Falstaff to carry the name of a real person, Sir John Oldcastle. A knight who had fought beside the real Henry V, Oldcastle was nothing like Falstaff, so when his descendants got wind of Shakespeare's intent, they complained. One of them was an official censor, leaving Shakespeare with no choice but to change the name or be banned. In typical fashion, however, he got the last word by inserting a few "old castle" jokes into his script. Prince Hal refers to Falstaff at one point as "my old man of the castle."

The role of Falstaff has long been considered a plum. Actors—and actresses—have clamored to play it. Anthony Quayle, Orson Welles, and

Ralph Richardson have all been Falstaff; so has Pat Carroll, who transformed herself into the portly has-been knight for a 1990 production at the Folger Shakespeare Library in Washington, D.C.

THE COMEDIES

Shakespeare's thirteen comedies are sophisticated, complicated, farcical, slapstick, and even a bit tragic. We love them for the glimpses they give of foolish humans triumphing over adversity in surprising ways.

~ 76 ~
Not exactly standup

If you come to a Shakespearean comedy expecting to see a Neil Simon play with funny costumes, you're bound to leave disappointed. What made people laugh in Shakespeare's time was different from what we find funny today. For Elizabethans, escaping into a fanciful world of mischievous fairies and men cavorting as women cavorting as men was reason enough to shell out a precious penny for an afternoon at the theater.

The audiences who came to see Shakespeare's comedies could expect to hear plenty of wordplays, puns, and quibbles. A quibble was a kind of verbal game of one-upsmanship, in which opponents try to squeeze as many meanings as possible from a single word while engaging in clever repartee. Topical humor—jokes and allusions to famous people or events of the day—was especially popular. A favorite running gag centered on cuckolding. A man whose wife was unfaithful was labeled a cuckold; he was susceptible to growing horns. In Elizabethan times, even a casual reference to horns or to an animal, such as a deer or a goat who sported them, could send an audience into frenzied hysterics. (Not much different from the frenzied hysterics of a sitcom's laugh track when body parts are mentioned—Shakespeare wasn't above using the lowest common denominator.)

But Shakespeare's comedies were more about illusion than slapstick. The humor was often subtle, couched in improbable situations, deceptions, and misapprehensions, usually involving lovers, lost children, identical twins, or women disguised as men. The eventual outcome would always be happy (or at least not tragic), but getting there could often be dicey.

There's a good deal of darkness in a Shakespeare comedy. In several of them, one of the leading characters is under threat of death. In the opening scene of *A Midsummer Night's Dream*, Hermia is offered three fates: marriage to a man she doesn't love, banishment to a convent, or death. Some choice, eh? Not exactly stuff that leaves an audience rolling in the aisles. In *Measure for Measure*, one of the dark comedies, the protagonist Claudio spends much of the play under sentence of death.

But that's precisely the point. Comedy, as opposed to tragedy, in Shakespeare's day meant that the threatened character would eventually be saved. In the meantime, any anxiety the audience might feel over his or her possible fate was deliberate and simply part of the comedic pattern. Comedies weren't devoid of tragedy; they just handled it in a more lighthearted manner. In the end, the shrew would be tamed, enemies would become friends, villains would undergo miraculous conversions, and everyone would go home satisfied.

~77~
Fitting square pegs into round holes

With all its deception, disguises, and madcap antics, it's easy to figure out that a play like *Twelfth Night* should be classified as a comedy. You get into trouble when you to try to categorize a play that has elements of farce on one page and tragic battlefield scenes on the next. Such is the case with three of Shakespeare's alleged comedies—*All's Well That Ends Well*, *Measure for Measure*, and *Troilus and Cressida*. These three plays have posed such problems to scholars who tried to fit them into the traditional classifications they finally designated them as "problem plays."

Although all three plays have comic elements, some are so darkly satirical it's difficult to find much to laugh about. In this day and age, these plays might be called "black" or "absurd" comedies. They make us laugh, but they sure don't improve our outlook on the world.

All's Well That Ends Well is peopled with characters who are hardly endearing—a woman who tricks a man into living with her by getting pregnant and a man who agrees to marriage because his only other choice is jail. This is hardly the stuff of which happily-ever-afters are made. The characters in *Measure for Measure* aren't much more admirable. There's the strict moralist who propositions a beautiful young virgin, the brother who convinces his sister to trade her virtue for his life, and the duke who disguises himself as a monk in order to spy on the town to determine where his shortcomings as a ruler lie. Along the way, there's an ordered execution and a couple of forced marriages. This is supposed to be funny?

Troilus and Cressida, with its overall sense of gloom and the futility of life, is especially troubling. When it was published as a quarto in 1609, the title page called this classic tale of love and war in Trojan times a history; an advertisement attached to some copies of the quarto called it a comedy. Unsure of exactly how to classify it, the editors of the *First Folio* placed it between the histories and tragedies and labeled it "The tragedie of Troylus and Cresside." They were right to be confused. The characters aren't particularly sympathetic, and it doesn't fit into any traditional genre. Perhaps its most outstanding quality is that it demonstrates how Shakespeare could take a genre like comedy and stretch it to suit his needs by incorporating tragic elements you wouldn't expect to find there.

To understand the problem plays, we should look at the context in which they were written. All three date to approximately 1603, the year Queen Elizabeth died and James I ascended to the throne. Perhaps the pessimism we see on the stage is a reflection of what was going on outside the London theater at the time they were first performed.

~78~

Walking the fine line between comic and tragic

As a product of his age, Shakespeare knew comedy and tragedy were more alike than they were different. The only thing that sets a comedy apart from a tragedy is that in comedy, the ending is always happy; no one dies. Still, for a comedy to succeed onstage, it can't be just a running gag. It must incorporate some tragic elements, too. And Shakespeare was a master at providing them.

Shakespeare's comedies always begin as potential tragedies. With a simple misunderstanding. Or a feud. Or a seemingly insurmountable obstacle. At the opening of act one, the situation looks bleak. But by the time the play is over, disaster has been averted by the actions of a plucky heroine or the grace of some benevolent fairy or god. Freedom and playfulness are the hallmarks of Shakespearean comedy.

While tragedy's focus is narrow and fiercely intense, centered largely on one person and his struggles against a deeply ingrained flaw, comedies take a broader view. Change is inevitable and human beings must cope with it together, as couples or in groups. Thus, Shakespeare's finest tragedies are named for individuals such as Hamlet, Othello, or Macbeth, whereas his comedies might take their titles from holidays (*Twelfth Night*) and mysterious doings after dark (*A Midsummer Night's Dream*). And while comedies are not without problems or barriers, the solutions are usually obvious and always within easy reach—as soon as the characters open their eyes.

In a comedy, a protagonist might pretend to be dead, but in the end he is revived. In a tragedy, disaster is inevitable. Comedies end in marriage, or at least the promise of it. Tragedies end in death. Tragic characters must accept the responsibility for their actions; for comic characters, there's always a second chance. And even though life inside a comedy can sometimes seem menacing, from the perspective of an audience, there's always the comforting feeling that everything will eventually be okay.

Nowadays everyone knows that *Romeo and Juliet* is a tragedy, but it feels like a comedy throughout much of its duration, except for the announcement by the Chorus at the beginning that "A pair of star-crossed lovers take their life." Romeo begins the play spouting bad poetry about Rosaline, who is soon quickly forgotten when he sees Juliet. And the witty speeches of Mercutio and the Nurse, among other characters, are quite reminiscent of the comedies. In fact, even the complicated death plots seem more like comedy than tragedy until the audience really knows the protagonists are dead. Maybe Shakespeare even wrote the play as a comedy and then—who knows why—decided to kill off the "star-crossed" pair.

~*79*~

When gender reversal was a cause for guffaws

My, how times change. In twenty-first-century America, the whole idea of cross-dressing is a politically correct hot potato. In Shakespeare's time, women dressing up as men, and vice versa, on the stage was cause for hilarity and a clever dramatic device often used to drive an important point home.

In Elizabethan England, audiences knew that men played women's roles onstage and that when a woman, played by a man, disguised herself as a man during the course of a play, something funny was about to occur. Shakespeare delighted in exploring the meanings of the terms feminine and masculine. To Shakespeare's way of thinking, cross-dressing implied that the matter of gender was not to be taken too seriously. By disguising themselves as men, female characters could do and say things they might not otherwise be able to. The barriers that existed between men and women came crashing down when clothing was exchanged.

Disguised as a man, a woman could feel freer than she'd ever felt before. Suddenly, an adventurous woman could safely navigate an otherwise dangerous world on her own. She could secretly test the fidelity of her mate. And she could, for perhaps the first time ever, speak openly with a member of the opposite sex, unfettered by the traditional rules of courtship that governed the personal relations between men and women in Elizabethan times.

And so we see many of Shakespeare's comic heroines donning men's clothes: Portia in *The Merchant of Venice*, Viola in *Twelfth Night*, Rosalind in *As You Like It*. Every one of them appears in "drag." It's all part of Shakespeare's plan to fashion a world in which the boundaries between player and part, reality and mirage, become blurred.

~ 80 ~

What's so funny about Shylock?

Not a darn thing. *The Merchant of Venice* is considered a comedy because it has a happy ending. And happy endings in Shakespeare's time didn't mean that everyone—least of all a Jewish villain—would be treated fairly or well. Midway through this play, when things are looking especially bleak for Antonio, we wonder if the villain might just this once prevail. But this is a comedy, remember, and so in the end, Portia wins the heart of Bassanio, Antonio's ships really do come in, and Shylock doesn't get the chance to extract his pound of flesh after all.

What is interesting about this play, at least from a sociological point of view, is its portrayal of a Jew. Anti-Semitism ran rampant in Elizabethan England, and if Jews were depicted onstage at all, it was usually as greasy, hook-nosed moneygrubbers. In that regard, Shakespeare's

Shylock is just slightly off the mark. He is by no means sympathetic, but he doesn't exhibit the Machiavellian qualities of Christopher Marlowe's Barabas in *The Jew of Malta,* either. To be sure, Shylock is the quintessential anti-Semitic caricature of a Jew. However, you get the idea that his intense dislike of Antonio is not simply unjustified anti-Christian sentiment. Antonio has not only spit on Shylock and called him names ("dog" and "cutthroat Jew"), but the ruthlessly ambitious Venetian has cut into Shylock's money-lending business by offering interest-free loans. Shylock's determination to recoup his losses seems justified, although his vengeful plot and refusal to consider an ounce of mercy do not. As Shakespeare often does in his plays, he shows great understanding for a position that his play ultimately shows is unsupportable.

There is the eloquence, too, that Shakespeare allows Shylock to display. When he finds out that his daughter, who has run off with Antonio's friend, has traded his dead wife's ring for a monkey, he says, "I would not have given it for a wilderness of monkeys," and the audience can't help but sympathize, especially after just hearing his "Hath not a Jew eyes?" speech. No wonder that over the centuries some of the world's greatest actors have clamored to play Shylock. Some have performed the role as a traditional villain, others, as a quasi-sympathetic antihero.

In his portrayal of Shylock, Shakespeare broke with convention. His Jew was not the figure of absolute evil; still, he is a comic villain and we applaud his ultimate demise. Elizabethans would have likely seen him from a staunchly Christian point of view, as the epitome of all the qualities they had grown to distrust in Jews of the day. Our experience lends a radically different cast. In a post-Holocaust world, actors have chosen to perform the role in a much less antagonistic manner. In 1963, the Jewish actor Ernst Deutsch gave a groundbreaking performance in West Berlin of Shylock as a man alienated more by commercialism than by anti-Semitic sentiment.

～ 81 ～

Shakespeare's misanthropes

In an episode of the *Seinfeld* television series, Jerry persuades Elaine to attend a wedding with him by saying, "There are lots of people to mock at a wedding." Well, modern-day mocking may be fun to watch (apparently the large *Seinfeld* audience thought so), but as with most verbal endeavors, Shakespeare has a lot to teach us about mocking. Most of his comedies have observers who comment on the folly of their fellow characters—sometimes to the audience and sometimes in normal dialogue.

Some of the mockers are fools or other characters who also participate in the action. Some, like Benedick in *Much Ado About Nothing*, are major characters who "reform" from their misanthropy during the play.

Others, like Falstaff (see Number 75), are at odds with the play's themes, but might be more memorable than the characters who embody those themes. Even tragic heroes (Timon of Athens) and villains (Iago) can be effective mockers of mankind.

In *Troilus and Cressida*, Shakespeare even uses a misanthropic mocker named Thersites as the main commentator on the play's action. His presence is the reason many think of this play as a comedy; obviously, the events of any play named after two Trojans would normally make for tragedy. Have you ever thought an iron-fisted boss a fool? Then read Thersites on Ajax. Ever disliked a highly regarded personage's intellectual pretensions? Then listen to Thersites comment on Ulysses' idealistic speeches. He also likes to categorize different kinds of foolishness, even his own. Unlike fools in other plays, he seems to see almost all the action and comment on it, and subsequent events always bear out his cynical observations. In fact, Thersites disappears altogether just when the real action begins, never to return. Perhaps Shakespeare didn't need him anymore to make his point.

Make no mistake: Shakespeare was a great mocker of men and women. Unlike *Troilus and Cressida*, his other plays show up misanthropy and mockery as deficient ways to view the world (see Number 84), even as they do make many of the misanthropes—and their lines—stick in our memories.

THE TRAGEDIES

Shakespeare made this genre his own when he penned ten tales of otherwise honorable men and women who make the wrong decisions when they find themselves caught in impossible situations.

~ 82 ~

The shaping of a genre

The Greeks, from whom our great dramatic traditions come, had only two kinds of theater: comedy and tragedy. Distinguishing one from the other was simple. Comedy made you laugh; tragedy made you cry. In Shakespeare's day, the distinction between these two dramatic forms was not quite so cut and dried. Comedies could contain elements of pathos; tragedies could incorporate brief comic interludes to lighten the mood. Elizabethan comedies ended happily, usually with a marriage or the promise of one. Tragedies ended with death. And as these two dramatic forms continued to take shape and become more popular among Elizabethan theatergoers, William Shakespeare would be the one to put his special stamp upon the tragic genre. He would shape it, refine it, and ultimately make it his own.

Shakespeare wrote ten tragedies over the course of his twenty-five-year writing career. Four of them—*Hamlet, Othello, Macbeth,* and *King Lear*—are considered masterpieces, unequaled in the genre. His first tragedy, *Titus Andronicus,* written quite early in his career, was, from all accounts, a box-office success. Elizabethans seemed to love it, but not so with later audiences. Its graphic scenes depicting rape, mutilation, and cannibalism caused some scholars to question whether Shakespeare even authored this play. For centuries, it was considered too violent to be performed onstage.

Over the next five years, Shakespeare would write two tragedies, plus more than a dozen comedies and histories, before embarking on what would be known as his "Golden Age." From 1600 to 1608, he wrote seven tragedies, including the four for which we revere him most.

In many respects, Shakespeare changed the definition of tragedy for all time. While Aristotle spoke about the tragic hero's internal fatal flaw as the cause of his fall from grace, Shakespeare seemed to believe external circumstances played an equally important role. The young lovers Romeo and Juliet weren't simply "star-crossed"; the feud between their families triggered their destruction. Othello would not have acted as he did had the devious Iago not manipulated him—and Iago's enmity might not have been so great if his superior had been white. And as for Hamlet, the whole notion of avenging his father's death might never have occurred to him had the ghost not appeared and demanded it. Macbeth and Lear are shown as men who have a severe tragic flaw in the classic sense, but Shakespeare's depiction of the world around them indicates that the heroes' flaws are just a reflection of a flaw in society (or maybe even humankind) as a whole. In Shakespeare's tragedies, external events force otherwise noble men to make difficult and unwise decisions. What may begin as a miniscule fascination eventually blossoms into obsession, until these heroes spiral out of control, taking everyone and everything within their sphere of influence down with them.

Shakespeare's tragedies are eminently accessible. We know the deficiencies that drive these heroes because we see the same ones inside ourselves. Not surprisingly, the tragic heroes Shakespeare created have transcended time and place. Which is why, four centuries later, when we see them portrayed on the stage, it's as if we're still looking in that very same mirror.

~ 83 ~
Talk about baggage

When Shakespeare coined the phrase "bag and baggage" in his 1599 comedy *As You Like It*, perhaps he already had in mind the heroes of the four great tragedies he would write over the years to come: *Hamlet*, *Othello*, *King Lear*, and *Macbeth*. Talk about your baggage—these guys had it big time.

Although each faced vastly different circumstances and situations, these four men had one thing in common: They each had an area within themselves that was somehow deficient or flawed, and it reared its ugly head when each was confronted by a problem, mystery, or challenge. Hamlet couldn't make up his mind whether to kill his uncle in an act of revenge or to live his life without vengeance. Lear's inability to admit his mistakes drove him mad and killed even his only loyal daughter. Othello's unfounded jealousy propelled him to take one life and destroy his own. An unbridled lust for power caused Macbeth to commit an unspeakable crime.

When we hear the word *hero* these days, we tend to think of persons who, by their unselfish deeds, have demonstrated feats of courage or nobility of purpose. All too often we forget that heroes are simply ordinary people caught in extraordinary circumstances that push them to the limits of human endurance. When the choices they make are right, we exalt them. But when those choices are wrong, we label them tragic and turn away.

Shakespeare's great tragic heroes were not inherently bad men. They were good men of high birth and noble character who, when caught in impossible predicaments, made the wrong decisions and suffered the consequences. It's a fate that could happen to any one of us. And to quote a familiar phrase from Hamlet, "There's the rub."

What makes Shakespeare's tragic heroes so compelling is that we know they are somewhat like us (at least we'd like to think so). We may never be called upon to avenge our father's death, as Hamlet was, but we know what it's like to be suspicious or to lose a parent. And although most of us aren't murderers, we've almost surely felt the pangs of conscience just as sharply as Macbeth when we've done something to further our own ambitions. Looking at these four is like looking at ourselves . . . only magnified. They represent both the best and worst of humankind. Shakespeare knew what he was doing when he gave us Hamlet, Lear, Othello, and Macbeth.

In his other tragedies as well, Shakespeare gave the world more unforgettable tragic heroes than occur in most of the drama ever performed. In *Antony and Cleopatra*, Antony makes dying for love convincing, and it's fascinating to watch Coriolanus's pride bring him down below the level of those he scorns, even as we identify with him. Timon of Athens goes from believing too strongly in the goodness of his fellow man to becoming absorbed by a total hatred of mankind—who among us can claim never to have felt a tug toward one of those extremes?

From 1600 to 1608, Shakespeare wrote seven tragedies, and this period has been called his "Golden Age." Even though he spent more time writing comedies, we remember and most often quote his tragedies. Many scholars believe they are not only the finest English-language examples of their genre, but rank them among the greatest literary masterpieces of all time. Today, Shakespeare's tragic heroes still have something to teach us about our deepest desires and fears.

~ 84 ~
Now take a deep breath . . .

Any inexperienced writer is liable to break the rules of good writing because he doesn't know or understand them. The sign of a skilled writer is his ability and willingness to break rules he understands purely for dramatic effect. When it comes to breaking the traditional tenets of tragedy, William Shakespeare was more skilled than most.

Classical writers believed there were only two forms of drama—comedy and tragedy—and never the twain should meet. A comedy should be funny, but a tragedy should never make you laugh. Shakespeare knew better. Sensing when an audience needed a break, he went out on a limb and interjected a slice of comedy into highly charged tragic scenes, allowing his audience to take a collective deep breath when they most needed it and before he brought the house down. The great Greek tragedians would never have mixed comedy with tragedy. Shakespeare does it not only quite often but masterfully well.

Shakespeare's tragedies are full of comic interludes and delightful minor characters whose actions and comments minimize the intensity of otherwise impossible scenes. Who can forget the Porter at the gate in Act II, scene 3 of *Macbeth*? You could almost cut with a knife the sense of relief that washes over an audience when, just after Macbeth has killed the king, a loud knock rings out. That knock and the Porter's crusty comments about the effects of drink on sleep and sex break the tension and remind us that while Macbeth remains inside, as an isolated figure caught up in despair, outside the castle gates life must go on.

Then there's the devoutly loyal fool in *King Lear*. Like many minor characters in Shakespeare, he doesn't have a name. He's called simply "Lear's Fool." The Fool is what we would call a court jester; it's his job to entertain the king, but dramatically speaking, it's his job to tell his boss the truth. Some actors play this role as a comic one, but it's more than that. Traditionally, a court jester was allowed to speak more freely with a king than other folks, and Lear's Fool plays this part to the hilt. He is both funny and astute as he observes, and becomes a part of, the tragedy that befalls his master. As he casts his lot with the doomed Lear, he is reminded of his witticism earlier in the play: "Let go thy hold when a great wheel runs down a hill lest it break thy neck with following; but the great one that goes upward, let him draw thee after." He decides to ignore his own advice, though: "I would have none but knaves follow it, since a fool gives it." What a Fool for love!

An interesting aside about this part is that Lear's Fool disappears immediately after the storm scene and is not mentioned again. A likely explanation, held over from Elizabethan times, is that the comic actor Robert Armin played the roles of both Cordelia and Lear's Fool in the original production of *King Lear*. Since he couldn't be in two places at once, perhaps the Fool had to vanish so Cordelia could appear. In fact, when Lear carries out the dead Cordelia, he says "my poor fool's hanged!"

Is Lear merely confused, or is "fool" just a pet name for Cordelia? Or is Shakespeare, during one of the darkest moments of any of his plays, making a sly reference to the fact that the Fool and Cordelia are one and the same? Stranger things have happened in a Shakespeare play.

~ *85* ~
The enduring appeal of Hamlet

The renowned British actor Laurence Olivier once said, "*Hamlet*, in my opinion, is pound for pound the greatest play ever written." Apparently, a lot of people agree. (T. S. Eliot didn't like it, vastly preferring *Coriolanus*, but he's the exception that proves the rule.) No other play in Shakespeare's repertoire is so instantly recognized or so universally admired.

In the four centuries since it was first produced onstage at the original Globe Theatre in London, *Hamlet* has been performed more than any other play in the world. Its most famous line, "To be or not to be," is reputedly the most widely quoted phrase in the English language. *Hamlet* has been made into a movie no fewer than forty-five times and has been the inspiration for some twenty-six ballets, six operas, and several musical compositions by the likes of Tchaikovsky, Liszt, and Shostakovich.

Joseph Papp, founder of the New York Shakespeare Festival, used to tell his actors, "You haven't graduated until you've played Hamlet." Over the years a few hundred have stepped up to receive their diplomas, including the venerable Junius Brutus Booth and his son Edwin, Edmund Kean, Edwin Forrest, David Garrick, and William Charles Macready. In more recent times, everyone from Ben Kingsley and Mel Gibson to Ralph Fiennes, Harry Hamlin, Dame Judith Anderson, and Sarah Bernhardt has taken his or her turn at portraying the troubled Danish prince. Fat men, thin men, nude men, women in all shapes and sizes, an octogenarian, several dwarfs, and even a five-year-old acting prodigy billed as the "Infant Phenomenon of the Regency Period" have all played Hamlet. Shakespeare himself did not play this role; lead actor Richard Burbage would have likely been given that honor. Shakespeare did, however, appear onstage in *Hamlet* as the Ghost.

At 4,024 lines—1,503 of which are spoken by Hamlet alone—it is the longest play Shakespeare wrote and, as such, is rarely performed in its entirety. The uncut version takes just under five hours to stage. Under Stalin, *Hamlet* was banned in the Soviet Union. The official reason had to do with Hamlet's indecisiveness and depression, which Communist Party authorities deemed incompatible with the Soviet ideals of optimism and fortitude. Perhaps they'd seen the uncut version and were simply bored to death. In 1996, Kenneth Branagh made a film version of the uncut *Hamlet* with a running time of 242 minutes.

As if Shakespeare's own language isn't confusing enough for some modern theatergoers, Peter Brook staged a multilingual *Hamlet* at his

Théâtre des Bouffes du Nord in Paris in 2001. The production featured several leading international actors, including Adrian Lester as Hamlet, each speaking the lines in his or her native tongue. Amazingly, so familiar was the story that despite a garbled script combining English, Japanese, and Kiswahili, the audience seemed to have no difficulty following right along.

It's been four centuries since *Hamlet* debuted on stage, but there's no reason to think that interest in this play is about to die anytime soon. Groups of fans worldwide—called Hamletologists—have made it their mission to collect statistics about the play and to keep it forever alive. Shakespeare would be proud—or more likely just downright stupefied.

Why is *Hamlet* Shakespeare's most popular play? Well, it's got some great lines, but so do *Macbeth* and many other plays. It's got sex and violence, but not any more than most of Shakespeare's other tragedies. Perhaps the thing it's got going for it most is that there are lots of possible interpretations—and every new director thinks he or she has the key to understanding the Prince of Denmark. For years, most critics thought the main point about Hamlet was that he "couldn't make up his mind," as the Olivier movie states authoritatively at its outset, and in that movie, it's easy to see the root cause of his indecision from the way Hamlet stares at his mother's low-cut dress. Now that Freud's somewhat passé, other interpretations, many of a sociopolitical nature, have taken the fore. And as long as the interpreters keep trying, the rest of us will probably keep watching, because it's a great story, no matter how it's interpreted.

The Romances

While another writer nearing the end of his career might choose simply to rest on his laurels, only Shakespeare would reinvent himself with plays that combine the best of comedy and tragedy to create a whole new category called "romance."

~ 86 ~

A new twist on happily ever afters

Trust Shakespeare to keep reinventing himself right up to the end of his writing career. Sometime after his death, when scholars started to take a closer look at the last four plays he wrote on his own—*Pericles, Cymbeline, The Winter's Tale*, and *The Tempest*—they discovered something unusual. These plays didn't fit neatly into the categories used to classify Shakespeare's work. They certainly weren't histories, but they didn't seem like true tragedies or comedies either; they had elements of both. Still, history/comedy/tragedy were the accepted categories for Shakespeare's plays and so friends of the author and, later, serious Shakespeare scholars simply had to make these plays fit.

John Heminges and Henry Condell, compilers of the *First Folio*, were the first to do so. They put *The Tempest* and *The Winter's Tale* under the comedies, with the likes of *Twelfth Night* and *The Merchant of Venice*, and they relegated *Cymbeline* to the tragedies, alongside *Hamlet, Macbeth*, and *King Lear*. (They omitted *Pericles* entirely.) This classification stood for many years, but apparently, one day, some people got to reading the works a little more closely. They decided that these plays belonged in a category all their own. From here on out, they would be known as "romances."

To label a play a romance, especially one written by Shakespeare, could be tricky business. Romances were popular in Shakespeare's day, but they did not carry the weight of serious literary works. They were tales of knights and their ladies, laced with chivalry and amorous adventure. To this day, romances are considered frivolous, fine for escape on the commute home or to pack in the suitcase for a vacation at the beach, but certainly not works to be taken seriously. Could the man who, just a year before, had crafted the character of Macbeth be capable of such lighthearted whimsy? The answer is yes, because when it came to writing in any category, Shakespeare almost always broke the mold.

Just like his comedies, Shakespeare's romances contain young lovers. But instead of revolving around high-spirited high jinks, disguises, and playacting, the amorous antics of these romantic couples carry a hint of tragedy. The last scene may be happy, but it usually takes death, loss, or catastrophe to get there. *The Winter's Tale* is a case in point. The play opens with a jealous husband and a dead wife; it closes with their reunion. Shakespeare's romances tackle tragic themes: jealousy, death, disputes between parents and their children, not to mention big subjects like utopianism and imperialism (in *The Tempest*). What keeps the characters from descending into utter despair is their own resourcefulness. There are no soliloquies in Shakespeare's romances; characters come to self-realization through action rather than reflection. Past wrongs may not be forgotten, but they are at least forgiven. By the end of the play there's a feeling that whatever we hold most dear can never be taken away. The dead return to life and lost children are found. It's a switch from the tragedy genre that had so consumed Shakespeare for the previous five years.

Given that Shakespeare's romances came on the heels of his darkest tragedies (think *King Lear*), you can't help but wonder: Why did he decide to shift gears so abruptly? Several explanations have been offered. Perhaps he was bored with tales of gloom and doom, or maybe the birth of his granddaughter in 1607 transformed him in some way. (The romances do always involve some intergenerational reconciliation, in contrast to some of his earlier comedies, where the older generations may be excessively foolish or corrupt.) His first romance, *Pericles*, was written right about that time. Or maybe it was simply a matter of stagecraft. Shakespeare's acting company, the King's Men, was beginning to perform at Blackfriars theater, a more intimate venue than the Globe. Shakespeare's romances were filled with special effects—enchanted shipwrecks and statues that talked, not to mention the bear that appears in *A Winter's Tale*. Maybe Shakespeare was the Steven Spielberg of his day and simply wanted the perfect place to try them out.

~ 87 ~

Is that sprite a boy or a girl?

In *The Tempest,* Shakespeare invents an "airy spirit" named Ariel who acts as Prospero's willing servant. In Shakespeare's day, Ariel would have been played by a boy, since girls didn't play at all. In the present time, Ariel can be represented by either a male or female, and directors often make that choice based on what they want *The Tempest* to say.

The stage directions of *The Tempest* always refer to Ariel as "he," but the stage directions were almost certainly not written by Shakespeare. On the other side of the dispute, Prospero once tells Ariel to "make thyself like a sea nymph," a direction that it would perhaps be unmanly to give to a male, except maybe in Shakespeare's world of cross-dressing. Also, commentators on *The Tempest* throughout the centuries have noticed that Ariel acts very much like a muse to Prospero, and muses are usually female. Of course, when it came to gender, Shakespeare didn't always do the expected.

But the niceties of the script often don't motivate directors as much as the ideas they bring to the script. *The Tempest* is probably second to *Hamlet* in allowing for modern adaptors and audiences to bring their own meanings to it. Because it concerns the settling of a savage island by a European, many people, starting in the nineteenth century have viewed the play as a Shakespearean comment on colonialism and imperialism.

And of course it is, although Shakespeare's audiences would probably have been only marginally concerned about those topics. Also, because the play involves a father who keeps his daughter isolated from human society until her maturity, the play has been used by many who have something of their own to add to the ever-increasing public dialogue about the role of women in society. And, if you're making a point in sexual politics, it's important what gender you make somebody, especially if Shakespeare left the gender ambiguous in the first place. For instance, Ariel has been portrayed as a flamboyant homosexual to show the subservience of Ariel's natural freedom to patriarchal control, and as an Asian woman to show Prospero's colonial-type control over the character.

Clearly, Ariel can be whatever sex you want (him/her) to be. In one German production, Ariel was even made into a box of detergent (Ariel is the name of a popular detergent in Europe), thus skirting the issue altogether.

PART V

The Poems

Will you then write me a sonnet
in praise of my beauty?
—MUCH ADO ABOUT NOTHING

The Playwright Becomes a Poet

IF YOU WERE A WRITER who needed to make a living from your craft in Elizabethan times, you'd want to become a playwright. Writing drama was steady work, and it generally paid better than other writing. But if you wanted prestige, then poetry was the way to go. Writing verse could garner you respect from your peers, and if you were any good at it, a decent income to boot.

When the market for plays tanked—thanks to a "minor" complication called the bubonic plague, which closed the London theaters in 1592—Shakespeare turned to poetry and snagged himself a patron. Not only was he able to keep food on the table during an economic downturn, he boosted his reputation as well. In Shakespeare's day, poets were considered intellectually superior to playwrights. By the time he returned to writing full-time for the theater, it didn't matter that drama was still not considered a gentleman's profession. He'd made a name for himself as a writer and his future seemed secure.

~ 88 ~

Shakespeare a poet? No way!

Suppose you got to talking with a friend about Shakespeare. Don't laugh. It could happen, the conversation might go like this:

"So what did Shakespeare write?" you ask.

"Hmm, let me think. Um . . . oh yeah, I know. *Hamlet*. He wrote *Hamlet*. Oh wait, *Romeo and Juliet*. He wrote that, too. I think."

"Well, didn't he write some poetry, too?"

"Poetry? Nah . . . that was Wordsworth. Or maybe Keats. Shakespeare didn't write poetry. He just wrote plays."

Today, when you mention the name Shakespeare, you get the title of a play. In his lifetime, he was better known for poetry—by the reading public at least. And we're not talking just the sonnets here. Long before a copy of those personal declarations of love ever hit the London streets, the name Shakespeare was already on the lips of Elizabethan readers. Copies of his first narrative poem *Venus and Adonis* flew off the shelves when the work was first released in 1593. It was so popular that it had to be reprinted eight more times. A similar thing happened with his second narrative poem, *The Rape of Lucrece*. Published in 1594, it went into six editions.

Six editions? Of a poem? That's right. Elizabethans put poetry above all other forms of writing. Even Shakespeare himself viewed poetry with special regard. In the dedication for *Venus and Adonis*, he called the work "first heir of my invention," thus declining to acknowledge what had come before.

And what had come before was pretty darn good. *Henry VI, Parts I, II,* and *III, Richard III, The Two Gentlemen of Verona,* and *Titus Andronicus* had already played the London stage, and Shakespeare was making quite a name for himself. At just twenty-eight, he was well on his way to becoming a noted playwright, earning a steady income, and winning accolades in Elizabethan theater circles. Then disaster struck. Bubonic plague broke out in London, and to curb its spread, civic authorities closed all public playhouses. Shakespeare was out of a job. So he did what thousands of modern-day workers who are suddenly laid off do each year: He looked for a new way to make a living. And he found it, by writing poetry. Now, writing for public playhouses could hardly be called a gentleman's vocation. But poetry? Well now, that was an entirely different story. Even noblemen had been known to dabble in this fine art.

It wasn't as though he didn't already have some experience in the field. Much of the dialogue for his plays had been written in verse. Still, up until that moment, Shakespeare had considered himself a dramatist, and in terms of reputation, that wasn't necessarily such a great thing to be. Among writers in Elizabethan times, playwrights were the big moneymakers, but they weren't revered as artists; they were more like hacks, paid to produce on demand, and pretty close to the bottom of the social strata. Poets, on the other hand, were respected members of society. What poets lacked in earning power, they more than made up for in intellectual superiority, or so Elizabethans thought.

Of course, Shakespeare did have earning power as a poet. It probably didn't hurt the sales of *Venus and Adonis* when word got around that in addition to being elegantly written, the poem was pretty funny and downright erotic, too. Elizabethans loved a little titillation with their art. Loosely based on Ovid's *Metamorphoses*, it tells the story of a lusty goddess and her handsome paramour who would rather hunt than make love. Despite its tragic ending—Adonis dies, pierced in a particularly sensitive spot by a boar—the poem was an immediate success.

Within a year, Shakespeare published a second narrative work, *The Rape of Lucrece*. Longer and considerably darker than his first, it garnered equal acclaim and helped to cement Shakespeare's contemporary reputation as a gifted poet. The story, taken from an old legend about a virtuous wife violated by the son of a Roman king, was a familiar one that becomes more vivid and heart-wrenching in Shakespeare's hands.

Shakespeare wrote two more narrative poems—*The Phoenix and the Turtle* and *A Lover's Complaint*—but neither generated the buzz of his first two, which didn't seem to hurt Shakespeare one bit. By then, he was back to writing full-time for the theater. In the coming years, he would pen the plays that would seal his place in the memories of even the most casual readers worldwide.

~ 89 ~

A helping hand

When Shakespeare lost his regular gig as a playwright because of a bubonic plague outbreak that closed the London playhouses in 1592, there was no unemployment system to fall back on until he sold a poem. He needed a patron to support his writing "habit," and in 1593, he snagged one. Henry Wriothesley (pronounced "Risley"), third Earl of Southampton and Baron of Titchfield, stepped up to the plate to become Shakespeare's chief booster and personal meal ticket.

Lest you think Shakespeare sold out to some rich guy, think again. With the playhouses closed indefinitely, he simply had no choice. If he wanted to continue writing, he needed the steady income that only a wealthy, influential man could provide. Besides, among writers in those days, patronage was an accepted, even honorable, practice.

Wriothesley, or Southampton as he would have been called, was intelligent, ambitious, well connected, and at barely twenty years of age, younger than Shakespeare by almost a decade. He was good looking, too, in an almost effeminate way. A miniature of the earl painted by Nicholas Hilliard around 1593 shows a pale young man, clearly an aristocrat, with finely etched facial features and long blond hair. He had assumed the earlship at the tender age of eight, when his father died; Lord Treasurer Burghley, who served as his guardian, arranged for his education at Cambridge and later for his marriage. While barely a teenager, Henry had promised to marry Lord Burghley's granddaughter, Lady Elizabeth Vere, when he reached the age of consent (then eighteen) in 1591, but later reneged on the deal. Despite pressure from his mother, grandfather, and Lord Burghley, the Earl of Southampton said no; he wanted to be free. Free for what we can't be sure; however, there were rumors in the 1590s indicating that, for intimate relationships, he preferred men over women—although he later married a woman who was pregnant.

Thanks to Southampton's financial support, Shakespeare was free to try his hand at poetry outside of drama. In 1593, he published his first narrative poem, *Venus and Adonis*, to great acclaim. He hoped that his work would please Southampton. His dedication also promised to honor Southampton "with some graver labour," which turned out to be his second narrative poem, *The Rape of Lucrece*, published a year later. Shakespeare, now more confident than before in his relationship with his patron, wrote the "warrant that I have of your disposition, not the worth of my untutored lines, makes [the poem] assured of acceptance."

Whether Shakespeare and the earl had more than a professional relationship has been a topic of conjecture. Based on the study of Shakespeare's sonnets, likely begun in the early 1590s, many scholars believe the poet might well have been bisexual. He addressed the first 126 of these poems to a "Fair Youth," who many believe was Southampton. But if the poet and his patron indeed had a love affair, it didn't last long. By 1594, the London theaters had reopened and Shakespeare had resumed his career in drama. As far as we know, Shakespeare severed his relationship with the Earl of Southampton when he returned to the theater. At least the dedications in his subsequent works contain no apparent references to his former patron.

90

Autobiography? Yes, no . . . well, maybe

By definition, a sonnet is a personal declaration of love. So when Shakespeare penned 154 of them, we have to assume he was wooing someone real with his words—someone for whom he had amorous intentions. Therefore, Shakespeare's sonnets must be autobiographical.

Or not.

It could be that these poems were never meant to address anyone specific. Of all the arts, writing is perhaps the most personal. Even if Shakespeare had made no attempt at autobiography, it would have been impossible for the poet to edit himself out of his work. Everything he had ever done or known would automatically become fuel for his creative muse. So the object of his affection to whom these sonnets were directed must be a compilation of the loves he'd experienced over a lifetime.

Or not.

Maybe Shakespeare's sonnets were just literary exercises with no connection at all to his real life—merely the attempts of a neophyte poet to practice the sonnet form over and over again until he got it right. Or, better yet, a dry run for the themes of love and friendship he would depict onstage in later plays.

Or not.

Despite centuries spent combing his poetry and plays for clues, scholars have been unable to determine definitively when Shakespeare wrote his sonnets and to whom they were addressed. They're not even positive they've got the order right. The sonnets seem to tell a continuing story, but then again, who can be sure? While we'd all like to think that Shakespeare's sonnets shed light on his life, we just don't know.

And yet questions continue to plague us. Could he have loved a younger man and, if so, whom? Did a rival poet interfere with that relationship and, if so, who? Did some dark lady break his heart and, if so, who was she? Inquiring minds want to know: Were his sonnets the key with which, as William Wordsworth so eloquently put it, "Shakespeare unlocked his heart"? Or have we spent years searching for something that never existed in the first place?

Onstage, William Shakespeare was famous for his comedic farces. Maybe his sonnets were the biggest farce of all.

Or not.

91

Who were all these people?

If you read Shakespeare's 154 sonnets in numbered order from beginning to end, they seem to tell the story of a lengthy love affair in which
the author and three characters—a Fair Youth, a Rival Poet, and a Dark
Lady—loom large. If the sonnets were autobiographical (and that's still
up for debate), it would seem this trio must be drawn from real people in
Shakespeare's life. We'll never know for certain because he took the mystery of their true identities to his grave. Still, that hasn't stopped scholars
from guessing. Nothing like a little mystery tinged with scandal to get
the old literary tongues wagging.

It's widely believed that the Fair Youth to whom Shakespeare
addressed the first 126 sonnets is none other than his patron, Henry
Wriothesley, third Earl of Southampton (see Number 89). He certainly
fits the description the poet painted with words. Southampton was young
and handsome and, just as sonnets 1 through 17 imply, reluctant to marry
despite the poet's urging ("Thou art much too fair / To be death's con-
quest and make worms thy heir"). Whoever this Fair Youth might be,
the sonneteer is clearly smitten. He promises undying love, even when
the young man betrays him by sleeping with his mistress. Uh, excuse me.
Wasn't the poet doing a little betraying of his own?

Somewhere around sonnet 78, the story takes an ominous turn when another man—"a worthier pen"—enters the picture and begins to court our Fair Youth. Who was this Rival Poet? Many believe it was Shakespeare's old nemesis, Christopher Marlowe. A freethinker and a known homosexual, his talent came close to Shakespeare's own. Had he not died tragically at age twenty-eight, Marlowe might have achieved greatness himself. Other candidates for the position of Rival Poet include George Chapman, Samuel Daniel, and Barnabe Barnes. Who?

The Rival Poet disappears after sonnet 86 and everything appears to be going well for the sonneteer and his Fair Youth until number 127. Consumed for so long with his "lovely boy," the poet now turns his obsession toward a beautiful woman with melancholy eyes. Who was this Dark Lady? For years, the leading contender was thought to be Mary Fitton, a maid of honor to Queen Elizabeth I, later banished from court for sexual indiscretions after she became pregnant with William Herbert's child (Herbert, aka third Earl of Pembroke, resurfaces later in our tale). But portraits of Mary Fitton show her as fair-skinned and blonde, so unless the lady's darkness was entirely figurative, Mary couldn't be the Dark Lady.

On the other hand, a prostitute named Lucy Negro who was allied with the London theater scene just might be. So might Emilia Bassano, the teenage mistress of Lord Chamberlain George Carey, second Lord Hunsdon, the patron of Shakespeare's acting company. The Dark Lady also could have been a married woman associated with Southampton's household. Remember the mistress with whom our Fair Youth slept?

According to a recent theory, she might have been the wife of John Florio, the earl's language tutor and the poet's favorite afternoon delight.

Mary, Lucy, Emilia, Mrs. Florio. Is this complicated enough for you? Well, it's not over yet. When the 154 sonnets were first published in a single volume, another mystery guest made a cameo appearance. The 1609 edition of *The Sonnets of William Shakespeare* contains a dedication to "W. H." Now who the heck is that?

It could be William Hervey. Or is it Harvey? The name appears both ways in the few documents known. He married Southampton's mother in 1598; he might have been the one to pass Shakespeare's sonnets on to Thomas Thorpe for publication. Then again, W. H. could also be our good friend William Herbert, Earl of Pembroke, whose mistress Mary Fitton was for many years thought to be the Dark Lady. Or maybe it's William Hatcliffe. He acted at Gray's Inn, where *The Comedy of Errors* was first performed in December 1594, and Shakespeare might have loved him, too. Oscar Wilde seemed to think it was Willie Hughes, a boy actor who took women's roles in Shakespeare's plays. As proof, Wilde cited the line from sonnet 20, "A man in hue, all hues controlling." Oh yeah, that's conclusive. Well, at least these candidates had the right initials. Shakespeare patron Henry Wriothesley, the Earl of Southampton, another suggestion, had the right initials too, just in the wrong order. So maybe this was a trick.

Or an error. Could Thorpe have meant to write W. S. instead of W. H.? Maybe he just wanted to thank William Shakespeare for the privilege of publishing his work. Oh, but wait. Shakespeare might not have wanted such personal poetry published at all. If the work was unauthorized, maybe Thorpe meant for his dedication to say, "I'm sorry." If so, the apology went unacknowledged. And we'll never know for sure who any of these people were.

～92～

So what is a sonnet anyway?

Sonnets were all the rage in Elizabethan England. If a man wanted to woo a woman, he sent her a sonnet extolling her beauty and formally declaring his love. Considering that not every suitor would have had literary talent, imagine the amount of bad poetry this practice engendered.

Broadly defined, a sonnet is a lyric poem consisting of fourteen lines, usually in iambic pentameter, which follows a specific rhyming scheme. The challenge for any would-be sonneteer comes in choosing words that will best express his passion, then fitting them into this strict rhythmic structure. It's no easy feat.

Typically, sonnets fall into two categories: Italian and English, distinguished largely by their rhyming patterns.

Italian sonnets consist of two stanzas, one of eight lines (the octave) and the other of six (the sestet). The octave has two quatrains, rhyming ABBA ABBA. The theme is offered up in the first quatrain and developed in the second. The six-line sestet usually rhymes in one of three ways: CDE CDE, CDC CDC, or CED DCE. In the first three lines, the poet continues to ponder his theme, and in the last three he "resolves" it.

English sonnets, the kind Shakespeare favored, have four divisions: three quatrains, each with a rhyming pattern of its own, and a rhymed couplet, designed to bring the poem to a close. The rhyme scheme for an English sonnet is most often ABAB CDCD EFEF GG.

William Shakespeare wrote 154 sonnets in the English style, each titled simply by number. First published as a collection by Thomas Thorpe in 1609, scholars remain uncertain as to when, in what order, or to whom Shakespeare's sonnets were written. Since sonnets typically were directed at the object of one's affection and were meant to serve as private declarations of love, it would probably have been considered bad form to publish them at all. So while Shakespeare might have shared his sonnets with close friends, there is some question as to whether he ever authorized their publication. Over the years, the matter of reading such personal missives has been cause for comment. In her 1925 novel *Mrs. Dalloway*, Virginia Woolf writes, "Seriously and solemnly Richard Dalloway got on his hind legs and said that no decent man ought to read Shakespeare's sonnets because it was like listening at keyholes."

He makes a good point, although we, like all other lovers of literature, would be wise to ignore it.

Part VI

But Wait, There's More . . .

Although the last, not least . . .
—King Lear

Four Hundred Years . . .
and Still Going Strong

It's every writer's dream to be read and remembered. Perhaps no other has achieved this dream quite like William Shakespeare. At this very moment, someone, somewhere in the world, is either reading Shakespeare's work or performing it onstage. Many more people are repeating his words or being inspired by his themes without even knowing it.

Over the years, Shakespeare has given rise, albeit unknowingly, to everything from children's storybooks and Broadway spinoffs to acts of ecological disaster and backstage superstitions. Hollywood has cashed in on Shakespeare and so has the once quiet little riverside town he called home. Shakespeare is ubiquitous, all right, and you can't help but wonder what he'd think about that. If he had dreams of one day becoming rich and famous—and that's debatable—could he ever have imagined it would mean his face would be plastered on tea towels or his words spliced into magnetic poetry?

~93~
American idol

William Shakespeare may have been born in England, but America has had a long love affair with him, too. Although he never made it to the New World in his lifetime, in death he has popped up in the chronicles of U.S. history.

The first public presentation of a Shakespeare play in the New World is believed to have taken place on February 17, 1736, when *Richard III* was performed at the Dock Street Theatre in Charleston. Several Declaration of Independence signers, including George Washington and John Adams, were known Shakespeare fans, and both sides in the Revolutionary War adapted his words to state their positions. "To sign or not to sign—that is the question," wrote a loyal Tory about the oath of rebellion against Britain he'd been asked to endorse. Some rebels in New England countered with, "To be taxt or not to be taxt" in a Boston newspaper. During the occupation of New York in 1776, Clinton's Thespians, a group of British army-officers-turned actors, staged productions of *Richard III* and *Macbeth* for their redcoat compatriots to help pass the time.

As a young circuit-riding lawyer in Illinois, Abraham Lincoln carried his favorite Shakespeare play, *Macbeth*, in his saddlebag and later, as president, kept a copy of Shakespeare's works on his desk next to the

Bible and U.S. Statutes. Ironically, in 1865, a Shakespearean actor from one of America's most famous theater families, the Booths, assassinated him. Brothers John Wilkes and Edwin and their father Junius Brutus Booth had, just five months before, appeared in a benefit performance of *Julius Caesar* to raise money for a statue of Shakespeare later placed in New York's Central Park.

Long before Broadway became American theater's hub, many English actors came from across the pond to perform in Shakespeare's plays. G. F. Cooke, Edmund Kean, and William Charles Macready were favorites of American audiences. By the mid-nineteenth century, America had given birth to its own acting tradition and sparks began to fly between the opposing camps, each claiming to have better thespians. In 1849, the rivalry between fans of Macready and the American-born actor Edwin Forrest touched off a bloody riot that left thirty-one people dead in New York City.

Elsewhere in America, Shakespeare's plays were being performed in saloons, mining camps, town halls, and one-room schoolhouses, aboard wagon trains, alongside the swamps in Florida, and on the stages of Mississippi riverboats. In the 1840s, during the Second Seminole War, a band of Seminoles attacked an itinerant troupe of actors in Florida and made off with a trunk full of costumes. These warriors were later seen clad in clothing formerly worn by the likes of Othello, Hamlet, and Julius Caesar.

Americans loved Shakespeare for his flowery language and melodramatic plots. Given the tenor of their colorful political campaigns, they felt especially at home with some of his characters' bombastic oratory. When the poet Walt Whitman took to regularly riding down Broadway in a New York City omnibus spouting lines from *Julius Caesar* and *Richard III*, nobody blinked an eye.

So beloved was Shakespeare during America's early years, it probably wouldn't have surprised anyone to learn that he was responsible for saving at least one life on the American frontier. In 1764, as this story goes, an Army officer reported late to duty and missed out on an Indian ambush. His excuse? "I just lost track of time sir. I was floating down the river, sir, in my canoe, sir, reading *Antony and Cleopatra*. Sir?"

~ *94* ~
Be careful what you wish for

William Shakespeare has drawn legions of fans over the 400 years since his first play appeared on the London stage, and at least one of them may have taken idol worship a tad too far. The action one serious Shakespeare devotee took more than a century ago on behalf of his favorite author is still being felt across America.

Our story begins in late nineteenth-century New York with a drug manufacturer named Eugene Schieffelin. Schieffelin was a huge Shakespeare fan, and the more he read of Shakespeare's work, the more he noticed little details—like how many times Shakespeare referred to birds in his plays. Thrushes, skylarks, starlings—Shakespeare mentioned them all.

Well, that got Eugene Schieffelin thinking. The birds in Shakespeare's plays were ones the playwright probably would have seen each day outside his window in England. Wouldn't it be nice if Americans could see them, too? Schieffelin set about making it happen. No one had yet examined the ecological implications of transferring a species from one continent to another; there were no laws in place in late nineteenth-century America to prevent Schieffelin from carrying out his plan. So he went ahead . . . with gusto.

First he imported English thrushes and skylarks. With great fanfare, the birds were released into the American skies; but sadly, they did not take to their new environment. Within a few months, all had perished. Not to worry. There were still the starlings. In 1890, Schieffelin had thirty pairs of English starlings released into Central Park. A year later, twenty more pairs were released. The starlings seemed to like Manhattan just fine; at least they stayed in residence for six years, delighting turn-of-the-century New Yorkers by nesting in the eaves of the venerable Museum of Natural History. But then, just as many human immigrants of the period, Schieffelin's starlings (or more likely their offspring—starlings can be quite prolific) got the urge to head West and homestead. By 1928, they had reached the Mississippi River; by 1942, they were sighted in California. Today, starlings have made homes in every corner of America, from Florida to Alaska.

Starlings are extremely adaptable and apparently quite chatty. Relatives of the mynah, they often mimic the songs of other birds and can even be taught to repeat simple human sounds. ("I'll have a starling shall be taught to speak / Nothing but 'Mortimer'" says Hotspur in *Henry IV, Part I*.) If all they did was sing and scarf down garden pests, we probably wouldn't mind them. But they have some nasty habits, too. They reproduce at an alarming rate, drive off prettier birds, such as robins and bluebirds, feed on garbage, and defecate. A lot. They can even kill. In 1960, a flock of roughly 10,000 starlings got sucked into the engines of a Lockheed Electra as it took off from Boston's Logan Airport and caused the plane to crash, killing sixty-two passengers.

Over the years, attempts have been made to run them off with everything from artificial owls and electric wires to alarm systems and chemicals, but to no avail. Starlings seem to like it in America. Thanks to Eugene Schieffelin's romantic notions about bringing a slice of Shakespeare's world to ours, they're here to stay.

The moral of this story? Don't mess with Mother Nature. Or if you do, at least be careful what you wish for.

~ 95 ~
Pint-sized Shakespeare

If Shakespeare were alive today and writing for the movies, most of his scripts would garner at least an R rating. Some of the very qualities we adults love about his plays—the bawdy language and no-holds-barred references to sexual matters—are what make them unsuitable for tender young eyes and ears.

There's a dichotomy about Shakespeare's work that has troubled parents and educators for years. On one hand, we want our kids exposed to great literature at an early age; on the other, we'd just as soon they didn't read words such as *whoreson*, *prick*, and *copulation* too soon, mostly because then we'd have to explain what they mean and who feels comfortable doing that? Then, of course, there's Shakespeare's antiquated language. What new reader, just learning to cope with one-syllable words and ordinary subject-verb-object sentence structure, could figure out a line such as "Light, seeking light, doth light of light beguile." Even adults scratch their heads over that one.

For better or worse, some enterprising souls have tried to solve these problems by "dumbing down" Shakespeare's works. Two such attempts, both by sibling pairs from the early nineteenth century, stand out.

Among the first to tackle Shakespeare for kids was the brother-and-sister team of Charles and Mary Lamb. Their *Tales from Shakespeare*, first published in 1806, became a classic and can still be found on the shelves of most public libraries. In *Tales from Shakespeare*, the Lambs retell twenty of Shakespeare's plays as stories, skirting the so-called nasty parts but taking care to preserve as much of the original language as possible; Charles retells six tragedies, and Mary retells fourteen comedies. While this is Mary's only major literary work, Charles went on to become a renowned essayist, critic, and poet, well-known to crossword fans by his pen name, *Elia*. Because of its vowel/consonant pattern, the word *Elia* is a frequent answer in crossword puzzles, with "Lamb" given most commonly as the clue. His adult essays on Shakespeare and Shakespeare's contemporaries, along with *Tales from Shakespeare*, helped fuel an early nineteenth-century revival of interest in Elizabethan drama.

Another brother-and-sister team who tackled Shakespeare for children didn't take quite the same care. Harriet and Thomas Bowdler had grown up listening to their father read Shakespeare while carefully skipping over potentially offensive passages. As adults, they remembered this experience and used it as the basis for developing *The Family Shakespeare*, a ten-volume work that purported to add nothing to the original while omitting any words or expressions deemed unsuitable for family consumption. Published in 1818, *The Family Shakespeare* went largely unnoticed for eleven years, until the dawn of the Victorian era, when it became a household staple and was reprinted thirty times.

These stories, watered-down versions of the originals, leave out important details in many cases, for the sake of propriety. Unfortunately, a good deal of what makes Shakespeare special got lost in the process. For example, in the original, Macbeth says, "The devil damn thee black, thou cream-faced loon! Where got'st thou that goose look?" In the Bowdlers' version, the Scottish king's words are reduced to, "Now friend, what means thy change of countenance?" Likewise, Hamlet's reference to his mother's "incestuous sheets" gets eliminated altogether, thus leaving out an important indication of Hamlet's feelings about his mother's remarriage. The Bowdler siblings and their wholesome brand of Shakespeare are no longer with us, but their names are immortalized in a word we sometimes still use today. Dictionaries define the term *bowdlerization* as the striking out of offensive material. Looks like even in death, Shakespeare has contributed to our language.

~96~
Hooray for Hollywood!

Once Thomas Edison filed for his patent on the first motion picture camera in 1891 and the industry took off, it was only a matter of time before Shakespeare made the move from stage to screen. In 1899, Herbert Beerbohm released the first film from Shakespeare—a brief silent clip of the dying scene from *King John*—and the race was on. During the first three decades of the twentieth century, seventeen Hamlets, ten Julius Caesars, eight Macbeths, and ten merchants of Venice made their way onto America's movie screens. These silent movies of course contained few Shakespearean lines.

Talking films of Shakespeare's work were slow to catch on, perhaps because of the unfamiliar dialogue, but once directors figured out that films gave them the chance to shoot huge crowd scenes in realistic locations, it was off to the races again. Among the early offerings were a 1935 film of *A Midsummer Night's Dream* by Max Reinhardt and William Dieterle and George Cukor's 1936 production of *Romeo and Juliet*. (Some people point to these movies as proof that not even Hollywood can ruin Shakespeare.) A British-made movie of *Henry V*, starring Laurence Olivier, was especially well received. Filmed in war-torn London during 1944, it featured a reconstructed Globe Theatre for its opening and closing scenes. More important, it depicted a triumphant English invasion of France. A seasoned Shakespearean actor onstage, Olivier also starred in acclaimed motion picture productions of *Richard III* (1956) and *Othello* (1965). His portrayal of the tragic Moor garnered him an Oscar nomination; costars Maggie Smith as Desdemona, Frank Finley as Iago, and Joyce Redman as Emilia were also nominated for Academy Awards.

Joseph Mankiewicz's 1953 film of *Julius Caesar*, starring John Gielgud as Cassio and Marlon Brando as Marc Antony, drew critical acclaim as well. Franco Zeffirelli also had good luck when he directed Richard Burton and Elizabeth Taylor in his production of *The Taming of the Shrew* in 1967. A year later, Zeffirelli scored a big hit with teenage moviegoers when he cast the very young Olivia Hussey and Leonard Whiting in a Verona-based version of *Romeo and Juliet*. A 1996 film of the same work, starring Leonardo DiCaprio and Claire Danes, placed the lovers in gang-ridden, postmodern Los Angeles.

Other notable recent movie adaptations include the 1999 film of *Othello*, starring Laurence Fishburne in the lead role and Kenneth Branagh as Iago; a 1996 motion picture production of *Hamlet*, featuring Kenneth Branagh, Kate Winslet, Derek Jacobi, and Julie Christie; and the 1993 *Much Ado About Nothing*, in which Kenneth Branagh, Emma Thompson, Denzel Washington, and Keanu Reeves frolic their way across Tuscany. Perhaps less notable is Kenneth Branagh's recent movie version of *Love's Labour's Lost*, which just goes to show that even Shakespeare can't *always* keep a movie from flopping.

Some of the most interesting and successful Shakespeare-related movies haven't re-created his works at all; they've been built around them. *The Dresser*, a 1983 film starring Albert Finney and Tom Courtenay, tells the story of a fading star and his fussy and also fading dresser from behind the scenes at a traveling troupe's production of *King Lear*. In George Cukor's 1948 film *A Double Life*, Ronald Colman gives an Academy Award-winning performance as an actor who starts to confuse real life with his stage role of *Othello*. In the 1977 Neil Simon comedy *The Goodbye Girl*, Richard Dreyfuss plays a young actor struggling to portray one director's vision of Richard III as a drag queen with a lisp. The movie-making team of James Ivory and Ismail Merchant got its start with a film about a troupe of actors performing Shakespeare in India—Shakespeare has gotten around the former British Empire, not to mention he's the most-performed dramatist in Germany.

Periodically, even Broadway got into the adaptation act. The musicals *West Side Story*, *Kiss Me Kate*, and *The Boys from Syracuse* were loosely based on *Romeo and Juliet*, *The Taming of the Shrew*, and *The Comedy of Errors*, respectively.

The most recent popular Shakespeare-related spinoff is the 1998 film *Shakespeare in Love*, which tells the make-believe story of a young Will Shakespeare and his mistress, set against the writing of and rehearsals for the original production of *Romeo and Juliet*. The fact that this film won seven Academy Awards, including Best Picture and Best Actress for Gwyneth Paltrow, says something about William Shakespeare's enduring nature and our modern-day interest in the intimate details of his life . . . even if those details are pure fantasy.

～*97*～
Beware the dreaded "M" word

If you've ever seen a live production of *Macbeth* and lived to tell about it, consider yourself fortunate. So much bad luck has been associated with this play, it's a wonder theater producers can get anyone to put it on.

Bad stuff began to happen the minute this play took to the stage. During its premiere performance on August 7, 1606, Hal Berridge, the boy actor cast as Lady Macbeth, collapsed from a fever and died backstage. Rumor has it that Shakespeare himself stepped in to fill the void. Considering he was forty-two and allegedly sporting a full beard by then, this story seems a stretch. Still, the show must go on. Things did, however, go downhill from there.

In 1703, on the afternoon a production of *Macbeth* was slated to open in London, the city was hit by a freak snowstorm, one of the worst ever recorded in England. Queen Anne blamed the play and ordered all theaters shut down for a week of prayer and repentance. Across the pond, in New York City, fans of the American-born Edwin Forrest became upset in 1849 when they learned their idol would not be playing the part of Macbeth at an Astor Place Opera House production. The star instead would be British actor Charles Macready. A riot broke out on opening night, May 10, and before the Seventh Regiment and four cavalry companies could bring it under control, thirty-one people lay dead. These people took their theater seriously.

On April 9, 1865, during a cruise along the Potomac with friends, President Abraham Lincoln is said to have read aloud from his favorite play, *Macbeth*. Five days later, actor John Wilkes Booth assassinated him. Booth's father, Junius Brutus Booth, was famous for his portrayal of Macbeth.

Now fast forward to Harlem, 1936. At the height of the Depression, the government sponsored a production of the play, dubbed *Voodoo Macbeth*, which was set in Haiti instead of Scotland and featured an all-black cast. Audiences gave the production rave reviews, but New York *Herald Tribune* critic Percy Hammond, complaining it wasn't real Shakespeare and was a waste of government money, called *Voodoo Macbeth* an "exhibition of deluxe boondoggling." Several days later Hammond came down with pneumonia and subsequently died.

A year later, a production starring Laurence Olivier and Judith Anderson at London's Old Vic turned catastrophic. During rehearsals, a sandbag fell from above the stage, narrowly missing Olivier. The director and the actress who played Lady Macduff were involved in an auto accident on their way to the theater one day. Later, Snoo, the beloved dog of Old Vic manager Lilian Baylis, died. On the day of the final dress rehearsal, Baylis herself succumbed to a heart attack. Some twenty years later, just before another production of *Macbeth* opened at the Old Vic, a portrait of Lilian Baylis fell off the wall and broke into pieces.

Death, destruction, mayhem . . . with one common denominator—*Macbeth*. Could this be mere coincidence? Maybe. But theater people don't think so. To this day, you won't hear the *M* word or lines from the play uttered backstage at any theater. Ever. Sets, costumes, and props used for a production of *Macbeth* never appear in any other play. Inside the theater, actors, directors, and stagehands refer to *Macbeth* as "the

Scottish Play," "the Unmentionable," or simply "That Play"; everyone knows exactly what they mean.

Some believe the curse of *Macbeth* can be traced to Shakespeare himself, who deliberately tucked actual black magic spells into the three witches' incantations. Needless to say, this has never been proven. But should anyone inadvertently slip up backstage and say the dreaded word, the only way to break the spell is by ritual exorcism. The offender must step out of the dressing room, turn around three times, spit, and recite the line "Fair thoughts and happy hours attend on you" from *The Merchant of Venice*, then beg permission to re-enter. Ah yes, the show must go on.

~98~
Remains of the day

What's left of William Shakespeare? Aside from the house where he was born and his literary works, not a lot. According to the Shakespeare Birthplace Trust, which administers the author's birthplace and four other Shakespeare-related sites in and around Stratford-upon-Avon, no personal items can, without doubt, be said to have belonged to Shakespeare or his family.

That's not to say people haven't tried to claim they own a bona fide Shakespeare artifact. Over the years, several pieces of furniture have been pronounced "Shakespeare's Chair." To date, all have been found to be too new to substantiate such claims. In 1793, Thomas Hart, a descendant of Shakespeare's sister Joan Hart, passed a collection of Shakespeare "relics" to a Mr. and Mrs. Hornby, then the tenants/custodians of Shakespeare's birthplace. The collection contained a card and dice box, a sword, an iron deed box, an iron lock, and a firegrate. It is known that the widowed Mrs. Hornby took the collection with her when she was forced to vacate the birthplace because of a rent increase in 1820. She subsequently passed the items to her grandson, and some of them later showed up at an auction in 1896. The firegrate and iron lock, part of that sale, are currently on loan to the Shakespeare Birthplace Trust.

Also in the Trust's possession is a gold seal-ring bearing the initials "W. S." It was found in the early nineteenth century in the churchyard of Holy Trinity Church, where Shakespeare is buried. Is this mere coincidence or a real artifact? As tempting as it is to believe this is Shakespeare's ring, the Trust insists there's no conclusive evidence. The ring appears to be like those that would have been worn by a gentleman in Shakespeare's time, used to seal legal documents and letters. Surely, he might have owned such a ring, but no one can be certain.

Interestingly, although Shakespeare's will contains the words "I witness whereof I have herunto [*sic*] set my hand and seal," the document does not bear a seal. In fact, the words "and seal" have been crossed out.

Is that because Shakespeare never had a seal? Or because he lost his before he signed the will? If so, could this be it? We may never know, but isn't it fun to speculate?

~*99*~
Cashing in on Shakespeare

No other writer in history has generated quite the buzz of William Shakespeare. While plenty of people shy away from reading his work (too long, too old, too many big words), everyone who's made it to high school in America recognizes his name. In Britain, he's the only compulsory author in Advanced Level English Literature. So is it any wonder his hometown would look to his name for its economic well-being?

In Stratford-upon-Avon, Shakespeare spells business. Big business. Several million tourists flock there annually just to walk the same streets and breathe the same air as their hero. If you can get past the jolt of seeing the man's shining face looking back at you on everything from tea towels to pub signs, Stratford really is a charming place. The River Avon still meanders through town and there's lots to see and do . . . most of which is at least peripherally connected to William Shakespeare and some of which may actually be authentic.

The focal point of all the frenzy is, of course, Shakespeare's Birthplace on Henley Street. This half-timber house, headquarters of the Shakespeare Birthplace Trust, has undergone alterations since Shakespeare lived in it, but it remains a typical structure of the Elizabethan period. Shakespeare didn't sit on those chairs, nor was he necessarily born in the room that has been officially designated the "birth-room." The signatures of famous pilgrims, including Thomas Carlyle, Sir Walter Scott, Charles Dickens, and Mark Twain, who came to pay homage and etched their names into the windowpanes, are, however, authentic. Until 1847, the home was privately maintained and was rapidly deteriorating. A combination of the approaching 300th anniversary of Shakespeare's birth and the rumor that P. T. Barnum had his eye on the property and might be shipping it to America prompted city folks to fork over £3,000 to save it. With a per-person admission fee of around £7 these days, they've more than recouped their investment.

Within walking distance of the Birthplace are three other properties, also administered by the Shakespeare Birthplace Trust. Hall's Croft, a townhouse in the Jacobean style, was home to Shakespeare's elder daughter, Susanna, and her husband, Dr. John Hall. His dispensary is on view, along with examples of heavy oaken furniture from the period. Nash's House, home of Thomas Nash, first husband of Shakespeare's last direct descendant, granddaughter Elizabeth Hall, is heavily restored and open for visitors. Of particular interest is the garden where the foundations of New Place, the house in which Shakespeare died in 1616, can still be seen. Built in 1483, it was considered Stratford's second-finest home in Shakespeare's time and had once belonged to Sir Hugh Clopton, a former lord mayor of London; Shakespeare purchased it in 1597 for the whopping price of £60. Sadly, its then owner, Reverend Francis Gastrell, tore it down in 1759, in an apparent case of "I'll show you!" Previously, in a fit over the burgeoning hordes of sightseers coming to his property, he had chopped down a mulberry tree that Shakespeare supposedly planted himself. The townspeople stoned his house, and the reverend retaliated by tearing it down. So there!

Also of interest within Stratford are Holy Trinity Church—where Shakespeare, his wife Anne, and their daughter Susanna are buried, and where the parish register containing his baptismal entry is on display—and Guildhall, a Latin grammar school in Shakespeare's time. This building is still used as a school, and a brass plate indicates Master Will's seat.

Stratford's pride and joy is, of course, the Royal Shakespeare Theatre, home to the renowned Royal Shakespeare Company. Although the company itself has existed since 1879, the building is much newer. Completed in 1932 as a replacement for the first one, which had burned down three years before, its modernistic design has prompted critics to dub this place a "factory for Shakespeare." It is the site of almost always sold-out performances of Shakespeare's works throughout the winter and spring.

Two more Shakespeare Birthplace Trust properties lie just outside of Stratford. About a mile away, in Shottery, is the Anne Hathaway Cottage. With twelve rooms, this picturesque thatched farmhouse is hardly a cottage, but it is typical of the period and is the home in which Shakespeare's wife grew up. Mary Arden's House, the girlhood home of Shakespeare's mother, is located three miles from Stratford, in Wilmcote. It drew attention in 2000 when the Tudor farmhouse long thought to be Mary Arden's turned out to have been the home of the eminently unfamous Adam Palmer and was subsequently renamed Palmer's Farm. Not to worry. Research showed that Mary Arden lived in a house on nearby Glebe Farm; it has now assumed the title Mary Arden's House.

Shakespeare devotees also flock to Charlecote Park. Located four miles east of Stratford, this imposing estate, once the home of Sir Thomas Lucy, is reputedly the site of the infamous deer poaching incident that may have forced Shakespeare to flee his hometown for London around 1587.

⌁ *100* ⌁

All Shakespeare, all the time

If you're serious about studying Shakespeare, you don't have to go to England to do so. One of the richest collections of information and authentic Shakespeare memorabilia is as close as the Folger Shakespeare Library in Washington, D.C. Located within spitting distance of the Library of Congress and the U.S. Capitol, the Folger is home to approximately

256,000 volumes, centering on British and European literary, cultural, political, religious, and social history from the fifteenth through the eighteenth centuries.

The Folger boasts the world's largest collection of Shakespeare's printed works, including 229 quarto editions of various plays, seventy-nine copies of the *First Folio*, 118 copies of the *Second, Third,* and *Fourth Folios,* and approximately 7,000 other editions of Shakespeare's work, from a 1709 Rowe to the most recent Oxford, Cambridge, and Arden editions. Completing the Folger Shakespeare collection are hundreds of foreign editions of his poems and plays, plus about 1,000 prompt-books (alas, none dating to Shakespeare's time). The Folger also has thousands of theatrical playbills, programs, and scrapbooks as well as eighteenth- and nineteenth-century illustrations to Shakespeare works and portraits of leading actors and actresses from those days.

Visitors are welcome to view the Folger collections at no charge every day except Sundays and federal holidays. You won't be able to touch any of the books, of course, unless you can qualify to become a "Reader," a privilege for which you have to apply in writing, with letters of reference, to the librarian in advance. Access to the library's resources is limited to persons with a Ph.D. or equivalent degree, or graduate students who are writing their Ph.D. theses. If you don't meet these qualifications, you're not completely out of luck. Every year, on one day in April, when the Folger hosts its annual Shakespeare's Birthday Celebration, the Reading Room is open to all. (You can also get a free slice of birthday cake.)

The Folger is for serious Shakespeare devotees, but there's fun stuff there, too. The Folger Theatre stages periodic productions of Shakespeare's plays, and the library's shop, called Shakespeare etc., features Shakespeare-related apparel, games, gifts, posters, books, videos, and more. You can get a Shakespeare action figure, a mousepad with Shakespeare's face, jester hats, a ready-to-assemble model of the original Globe Theatre, bookmarks, temporary tattoos of William Shakespeare, a book of Shakespeare's insults, and a "Kill All the Lawyers" T-shirt (the Folger Web site touts this as a popular item, even though Shakespeare put it in the mouth of a ridiculous character).

In case you're curious, the Folger Shakespeare Library has been around since 1932. Its founders were Henry Clay and Emily Jordan Folger. Henry Clay Folger became interested in Shakespeare in 1879, when he paid a quarter to attend a lecture on the man by none other than Ralph Waldo Emerson (his ticket is part of the Folger collections). Around the time he married Emily Jordan in 1885, Henry Folger purchased a facsimile of the *First Folio* for $1.25. The book so fascinated him that he began acquiring the items that would later form the cornerstones for his library collection. In 1889, he purchased a real copy of the *Fourth Folio* (1685) for the whopping price of $107.50. Although Henry Folger did not live to see his library completed (he died in 1930), his widow Emily did. She remained involved with the library's administration and contents until her death in 1936.

101

What would Shakespeare say?

How is it that a man who wrote about kings, fairies, and star-crossed lovers more than 400 years ago still manages to entertain and inspire so many of us? There's no doubt he had a special gift, but from what we know of Shakespeare's life, it's safe to assume he had no idea he would become a literary icon. The details about whole chunks of his time on earth are missing, but it seems he was a pretty ordinary guy. A small-town absentee husband and father with average looks just trying to make a living in the big city in the best way he knew how.

That he was smarter than most is pretty obvious. He might not have had much formal education, but he had an ear for language and an eye for tales that would make good stories onstage. He was a hard worker; his literary output tells us that. He even managed to make a decent living off his writing, and thanks to a knack for the business of the theater, he was able to retire comfortably to his hometown. He was no doubt acquainted with some of London's leading citizens of his day—we know he performed before a queen and a king—but he never became one of them. In his own time, he remained forever connected to the shady world of theater.

The fact that he arranged to have his first two narrative poems published tells us he may have yearned for immortality as a writer, but he apparently didn't hold his plays in particularly high regard. At least he didn't try to publish them. His plays were not released as a collection until seven years after his death; many more years would pass before he became famous as a playwright.

It's unlikely that Shakespeare himself could have imagined the renown he would one day achieve. That those clever little turns of phrase he coined, often in a hurry to get them to the actors, would become ingrained in our everyday speech. That his own name would become the very "household word" he had described. That nearly 400 years after his death, on any given day, at any given time, someone, somewhere in the world, would be reading his work or performing it onstage. Or that millions of people would travel to Stratford-upon-Avon each year, just to walk inside the house where he was born. Surely, back in the days when he was struggling to create—writing and revising, then writing and revising again—he couldn't have conceived that one day people would read his words and dare to question whether he did the work himself or whether he even existed at all.

There are hundreds of things we do know about William Shakespeare, but there's still one really important thing we don't—and never will. If he could pay a visit to the twenty-first century to see what's become of his work and his name, what would he have to say?

INDEX